MANAGING THE AUDIT FUNCTION: A CORPORATE AUDIT DEPARTMENT PROCEDURES GUIDE

SUBSCRIPTION NOTICE

MANAGING THE AUDIT FUNCTION: A CORPORATE AUDIT DEPARTMENT PROCEDURES GUIDE
SECOND EDITION

Michael P. Cangemi, CPA, CISA

JOHN WILEY & SONS, INC.

New York • Chichester • Brisbane • Toronto • Singapore

REQUIREMENTS:
An IBM ® PC family computer or compatible computer
with 256K minimum memory, a 3.5″ high-density floppy drive,
PC DOS, MS DOS, or DR DOS Version 2.0 or later, and a printer.

IBM® is a registered trademark for International Business Machines Corp.

WordPerfect® is a registered trademark of WordPerfect Corporation.

Microsoft® Word for Windows™ is a trademark of Microsoft Corporation.

This publication is designed to provide accurate and
authoritative information in regard to the subject
matter covered. It is sold with the understanding that
the publisher is not engaged in rendering legal, accounting,
or other professional services. If legal advice or other
expert assistance is required, the services of a competent
professional person should be sought.

The first edition of this publication was entitled Corporate Audit
Department Procedures Manual.

Managing the audit function: A corporate audit department procedures
guide / Michael P. Cangemi.

ISBN 0-471-01255-6 (3.5″)

Printed in the United States of America

10 9 8 7 6 5 4 3 2 1

To my life's partner, Maria,
for challenging me to balance my
professional interests and my first priority—
my family: Michael Jason, Marc Ignatius, and
our world-class parents.

ABOUT THE AUTHOR

Michael P. Cangemi is Executive Vice President and Chief Financial Officer of Etienne Aigner, a member of the Hartstone Group, PLC. Before joining Etienne Aigner, he was Partner and National Director of EDP Auditing for BDO Seidman, where he created and directed a service area called Internal Audit Services. Prior to this, Mr. Cangemi served as Corporate Vice President at Phelps Dodge Corporation. At Phelps Dodge, Mr. Cangemi also held the position of General Auditor.

Mr. Cangemi has served as a principal at a major accounting firm where he was Director of the New York Office Computer Audit Program. He is currently serving as Editor in Chief of *IS Audit and Control Journal*; he is on the editorial advisory boards of the *Managerial Auditing Journal* (London) and the *Journal of Information Systems Security*. He is a member of the Board of Trustees of the Institute of Internal Auditors Research Foundation.

Mr. Cangemi has published many articles that have appeared in several publications including *Internal Auditing, Datamation, New Accountant, Computers in Accounting, The Practical Accountant*, and *The Internal Auditor*, in which he was recognized with the Outstanding Contributor Award in 1988. His contributions to books include a chapter in the *Handbook of EDP Auditing*. In 1991 he co-authored *Auditing in an EDP Environment* with Peter Reed. Among other honors, he has been a recipient of the Joseph J. Wasserman Memorial Award for Outstanding Achievement in the Field of EDP Auditing, and the Eugene M. Frank Award from the ISACA. He has also been listed in *Who's Who in America* and *Who's Who Worldwide*. In addition, he has given numerous presentations across the U.S. and abroad on a variety of topics related to audit and information systems control.

Mr. Cangemi received his Bachelor of Business Administration in Accountancy Practice degree from Pace University. He is a Certified Public Accountant in the State of New York as well as a Certified Information Systems Auditor.

CONTENTS

FOREWORD

At the turn of the century, copper mining companies such as Phelps Dodge Corporation were the darlings of Wall Street. They were growth plays at the dawn of the new age of electricity and communications. The demand for wiring throughout the country seemed endless. By the early 1900s, Phelps Dodge Corporation had already achieved a proud heritage. Formed in the early 1800s as a trading company, it wisely invested its profits in the copper mining business.

By the late 1970s when I joined Phelps Dodge Corporation as Chief Financial Officer, much had changed. I was asked by my good friend, then Chairman and CEO, George B. Munroe, to assist him and the Company in meeting the challenges ahead. The Management Information Systems (MIS) operating areas and the Internal Audit function were to receive special attention.

George and I found that the audit resource should be more consistently applied across company operations, and that the reputation of the audit function and the results of its efforts could be improved.

Michael Cangemi joined Phelps Dodge as Director of Internal Audit. My background as a Public Accountant and Chairman of BDO Seidman CPAs helped me to recognize the need for a strong internal audit function. Internal auditing is a difficult function to develop in a company. To allow it to contribute to the company, the internal audit management must be empowered with wide-ranging authority. The director of audit must possess integrity, initiative, and excellent communication skills.

Michael Cangemi had the personal traits we were looking for. In addition, he had a program to ensure that all audit personnel would be trained in the areas of information technology and the application of the technology to the audit function. Based on his work as Director, Computer Audit at the New York Office of Arthur Young & Company (now Ernst & Young LLP), Michael decided to integrate EDP audit and financial audit. His audit personnel team was designed to be capable of advancing with the Company into the information age.

Over the next two years, Michael proceeded, with the help of his audit team, to produce an audit methodology that resulted in a most successful audit function at Phelps Dodge Corporation. This book outlines the methodology that was implemented, and much more.

After those two years, Michael was promoted to General Auditor of Phelps Dodge Corporation. This was a high honor in a company that had a very lean corporate management structure. At the age of 33, he was one of the youngest officers in the history of the company. More importantly, he had gained the respect of the senior management team and the board of directors.

Procedures properly implemented produce the guideposts necessary to ensure that a function such as audit stays on course. Developing budgets for each audit assignment, preparing status reports, and planning documents are essential to efficient audit performance. Audit reports containing a summary report limited to two pages that give the scope of the report, key background information, and a conclusion and summary of findings in a concise bulleted format were created for directors. Detailed reports were prepared for use by those responsible for implementation.

Michael was fond of saying that "good people using good procedures will produce an audit product with a reliable, high-quality level." This was the result at Phelps Dodge Corporation.

Personnel development was a very high priority of the new audit program. Audit conferences were serious training and key team-building events.

The audit group was also assigned to activities such as contract, acquisition, and disposition audits. Contract audits alone have saved the company millions of dollars a year in contracting fees.

Once Michael had the audit function organized and had built a team that was capable of proper succession, he moved on to become a successful corporate vice president with responsibility for all of the company's information systems and benefit plans as well as internal audit.

You can take the methodology outlined in this book and improve your own company's audit program or use it as a basis for forming a new, modern audit program. Any chapter in this book provides ideas that are worth the price of the entire publication.

L. WILLIAM SEIDMAN, CPA
November 1995
Washington, D.C.

PREFACE

Who could find internal auditing interesting? Any smart internal auditor who pays attention!

Auditing is as exciting as the world in which we audit. In fact, anticipating and preparing for the changes that constantly take place in the business world makes auditing even more challenging. Coexisting with other management and partnering in the company's mission while maintaining a healthy dose of skepticism provides a significant interpersonal and intellectual challenge. However, many auditors live in a slow-paced, reactive world.

As a profession, internal auditing has been evolving for less than one hundred years. The Institute of Internal Auditors was formed in 1941 to fill a need on the part of the emerging profession's most astute professionals at the time. The profession continued to grow steadily through the 1950s and into the 1960s. The business community was changing dramatically, with technological leaps and global expansion leading the way. Internal control, as it was known, was destined to change to address the issues and complexities of the modern day.

The first wake-up call came in 1974 with the passage of the Foreign Corrupt Practices Act. Passed to address the practices of paying bribes in foreign countries, the law had requirements that adequate systems of internal control be maintained. Internal audit's role in management rose to new heights. The internal auditing professionals reacted swiftly and implemented new programs to strengthen internal controls and checks and balances. Those internal audit departments that were capable and proactive produced solid returns on investments for their organizations. Many branched out into operational audit areas that were heretofore only discussed. All audit functions addressed information technology in one way or another. Auditors met at conferences and shared information and best practices in a way that should be the envy of all professional groups.

During the past ten years, internal control has been redefined. The Committee of Sponsoring Organizations (COSO) issued its landmark definitional study of internal control. The product amounted to a five-volume publication which has, for the first time ever, attempted to define all of the intricacies and the subtleties of internal control and achieve agreement among leading professional organizations.

Currently, the profession is being examined as a candidate function for outsourcing. Is internal auditing a core capability? Can professionals from outside the organization perform studies of internal control without a thorough understanding of the personality of the organization? The debate on outsourcing is an interesting challenge for the profession of internal auditing.

During these decades, internal auditing groups that were proactive and worked hard to create excellent internal audit programs have continued to satisfy their management. They searched for new requirements, responsibilities, and ways to contribute to their organization. The first thing that all successful audit organizations have done is to organize themselves. It has always been my hope that this book would help audit departments improve their organization and operations so that they can improve their overall performance.

Internal auditing is a very challenging profession, and once the fundamentals of an audit organization are established through the development of a policies and procedures manual the audit department can focus more of its energies on the delivery of internal audit services.

This edition of *Managing the Audit Function: A Corporate Audit Procedures Guide* greatly expands on the prior edition. In addition to a general update, sections have been added for personnel performance evaluations, annual audit department meetings, information systems auditing standards, employee orientation and status reporting to management.

I am fascinated with auditing in general, and specifically the internal auditing profession. I first observed internal and external auditing as a member of the operations staff of a brokerage house in my college years. I then spent a number of years in public practice before joining a large corporation as Director, Internal Audit. After rising to General Auditor, I moved out of internal auditing and into a financial officer position. Internal auditing continued to report to me during this period, and I attended all audit committee meetings. I then joined a public accounting firm as National Director of EDP Auditing and Internal Audit Services. Currently I am the Executive Vice President and Chief Financial Officer of a company. There is little question in my mind that I have seen internal control and auditing from a number of interesting vantage points. My current position affords me one of the best views, from the standpoint of how internal auditing should fit into and contribute to an organization. All corporate managers have a desire to run a well-controlled operation. We need to be able to rely on the integrity of the data and the results of our operations. However, I am now further convinced of the need for the audit department to be proactive and to seek out ways to contribute positively to the corporate mission.

As pointed out in this book, the audit function does not have the same performance measurements available to them as do other line functions within the organization. I am also now more aware than ever of the need for cost justification for every dollar spent, especially dollars that are not spent in the direct pursuit of revenue. Internal audit departments must have the disciplines and measurements proposed in this book. These issues have come more clearly into view, and as a result of my current position I am certain that the methodologies suggested in this book are essential principles of internal audit management.

During most of my career I have been very professionally active. How else can one stay up-to-date on emerging issues? During the past two years I have been a member of The Institute of Internal Auditors Research Foundation, Board of Trustees. I previously spent four years on the IIA, Board of Research Advisors. My objective is to stay in a position to consider and study the emerging issues in the profession of internal auditing. This trustee position has given me the opportunity to work with the profession's leaders and study its issues. As a result, I have discussed some of the emerging issues, including outsourcing, self-audits and information technology developments in Chapter 1.

During my years as General Auditor of Phelps Dodge Corporation, I worked with a number of individuals who contributed, through their dedicated efforts, to the development of portions of this audit methodology. I acknowledge a large indebtedness to James Coffey, Jack Ennis, James W. Lee III, Russell Muller, and Chris Hendrickson. I would like to thank all of the professionals I work with at Etienne Aigner, especially Robert Chavez, our CEO, who demands excellence; Linda Kothe, our resident CISA and loyal associate who worked with me in public practice before joining me as our controller; and Barry Graff, our technology guru. I continue to be inspired by their dedication and their intelligence.

In addition, I would also like to thank my colleagues at IIA and ISACA who keep me connected to this interesting world of auditing. At IIA, Tom Johnson has been a special friend and supporter, my colleagues on IIA Research Foundation, Board of Trustees, especially Bill Hick, Bill Duane and Walley Pugh, who lead the profession in so many ways.

I would also like to thank my associates at ISACA who care so much about the profession's response to technological developments and who work to make *IS Audit and Control Journal* a contributor to the expansion of the professional literature. Finally, last but certainly not least, I'd like to thank Sheck Cho, my editor, who guided me through editions one and two, and is always there for support and encouragement.

Most of all, I would like to thank my family—Maria, Michael, and Marc—who tolerate not only my work and professional activities, but even my new hobby—my boat!

MICHAEL P. CANGEMI
November 1995
Edison, New Jersey

Managing the Audit Function: A Corporate Audit Department Procedures Guide

Chapter 1

MISSION

1.1 INTRODUCTION

It is the goal of this manual to assist you in developing your auditing function into a well-respected contributor to the company's mission. In order to achieve this goal, standardized procedures must be developed and followed by your staff.

Setting high standards will ensure that your department's work will be of sufficient quality to satisfy your mission and enable reliance by your independent auditors. Development of each auditor's individual professionalism can be greatly increased by understanding the company's expectations and being evaluated on compliance with approved departmental procedures.

This manual will serve to document approved departmental procedures. It will be the basis for establishing methods to ensure the highest performance and quality in the department. These procedures should be evaluated and updated on an ongoing basis to keep pace with changing conditions.

This book has been set up in the format of a procedures manual. Each page has a heading consisting of the company name, the title of the manual (Corporate Audit Department Procedures Manual, if appropriate), the section number, the revision number (if you choose to keep track of the number of changes made in a particular section), and the date of the revision. Much of the text has been written so that it can be considered boilerplate and be used with your modifications to easily create your own manual.

The manual is based on a methodology employed very successfully at Phelps Dodge Corporation. Subsequently, the methodology was used as a basis for audit management workshops and consulting projects. Through these processes, the material contained in the methodology was analyzed and improved over a ten-year period. The methodology is broken down into three main components: Mission, Chapter 1; Audit Planning, Chapter 2; Audit Performance, Chapter 3; Audit Reporting, Chapter 4; Personnel Administration, Chapter 5; and Quality Assurance and Marketing, Chapter 6. Chapter 5 contains sections devoted to personnel development, personnel files, performance evaluations, annual staff meetings, and new staff orientation. These are considered foundation administrative programs within any Internal Audit Department. Other programs can be added to your manual in this section.

Chapters 2, 3, and 4 each begin with a matrix that outlines the various tasks or functions addressed in that chapter.

(a) What Is Internal Audit Management and Why a Procedures Manual?

Internal Audit consists of people and procedures. In order to maximize the productivity of a group, the group needs a mission and consistent procedures to attain the departmental goals. This procedures manual provides a place to state the department mission and document departmental procedures to attain that mission. All people need a mission. They also need goals—short-term and long-term—that can be linked to the mission. Other elements of management include feedback and mentoring, resources and training, and rewards. These elements can all be documented in a procedures manual.

We have said that Internal Auditing involves people and procedures. In most cases, the procedures involve reviewing and evaluating controls, efficiency, effectiveness, and other aspects of the business. This review process creates at least two factors for audit management to consider. The first is the difficulty in measuring internal audit productivity, and the second factor relates to the potentially negative nature of the auditing business. Both of these factors must be addressed in a progressive Internal Audit Department.

Auditor productivity requires the development of a proactive spirit, a high degree of professionalism, and measurement techniques, including budgets and time reporting. The methodology contained in this Manual includes a conscientious attempt to address all of these areas. Budgets are important. Time reporting—although a laborious task—is necessary to properly analyze audit productivity. A proactive spirit and professionalism must be instilled in all staff members through the department's professional development program.

Auditors can reach beyond the negative aspects of the auditing business. A modern audit department proactively seeks positive deliverables from within the work of the organization. This may involve the development of preventive control procedures, and the recommendation of these to auditees before audits. The overarching goal of the audit program should be to improve the control environment within the company. It should *not* be to catch company units or individuals in violation of control procedures. It is critical that the Audit Department develop a "work with" attitude within the organization.

(b) Essence of Internal Auditing

One of the major challenges of audit management is contributing to the organization's mission. It is often noted that internal auditors do not create, make, find, or deliver the organization's products or services. How does internal audit fit into the organization's mission? If audit programs were suspended, what would be the short- and long-term effects?

Company management will periodically examine the contribution of the internal audit program. Will your function pass the test? Unlike functions that produce products or services, audit results may be more difficult to measure. How is productivity of the internal audit function measured? Does your audit function have the internal system to measure and improve internal audit productivity? Other areas are monitored and pushed to greater limits; why not internal audit?

All too frequently, audit management becomes lax. Decisions to spread out and space out audits are all too easy. These types of issues do not exist in other functions—shipping is measured monthly, sales sometimes daily, accounting reports are issued monthly. With audit management comes the responsibility to push for greater volume, efficiency, and effectiveness. Audit management needs to employ any and all tools and procedures to measure and improve productivity. All of these procedures and methodologies should be carefully developed, documented in your procedures manual, and built into your audit culture.

What happens if you become lax? Management does not look at internal audit every day, month, or quarter. Over time, an impression is recorded on the effectiveness and efficiency of the internal audit function. In many cases, change is made in dramatic fashion by changing audit management; by eliminating, reducing, or outsourcing the function. The fact that all appears quiet may be only a warning for an impending storm.

(c) Quality Assurance Reviews of Internal Audit

Recently, quality assurance reviews of internal audit functions have been on the rise. This internal or external review is a very positive development. To some extent, this trend is encouraged by the very nature of the essence of internal audit and the concern on the part of management about internal audit effectiveness and efficiency.

Every dollar spent on internal audit is a dollar not earned on the bottom line. Why not challenge the spending, as is the case in other areas of the company? (Chapter 6 proposes a full Quality Assurance Program administered by audit management.)

(d) Outsourcing Internal Audits

A recent manifestation of the concern of management about the effective use of corporate resources for internal auditing is the ever-expanding trend toward outsourcing the internal audit function.

As noted earlier, internal auditing management requires a proactive approach, good personnel, personal development programs, structured procedures, a mission, short- and long-term objectives, quality assurance reviews, productivity measures, and so forth. However, there is no simple measurement tool such as units booked, units shipped, financial statements produced on time with accuracy every month, same store sales vs. last year, capacity utilization, etc.

Audit contribution is very difficult to measure! Therefore, when management is offered a simple, perhaps less expensive approach, it will be seriously considered. Is internal audit an organization's core competency? Can it be more efficiently and effectively implemented by an organization dedicated to internal audit as a core competency? These are questions currently being explored by many organizations.

Clearly, there are many factors involved in the decision to outsource all or part of an internal audit function. A major element is size and ability to maintain various specialized skill sets such as information systems (IS) audit. In smaller organizations, outsourcing of general IS audit may be effective and efficient. In larger organizations, with IS audit staffs, outsourcing certain very technical audits may be the advisable course of action. Outsourcing should be considered during the departmental planning process.

Recently, The Institute of Internal Auditors has issued a "Perspective on Outsourcing Internal Auditing." The IIA takes the following view:

> The IIA's perspective is that internal auditing is best performed by an independent entity that is an integral part of the management structure of an organization. The IIA states unequivocally that a competent *internal* auditing department that is properly organized with trained staff can perform the internal auditing function more efficiently and effectively than a contracted audit service.

> Internal auditing *by definition* should be internal and integral to the organization, and the internal auditing department should be staffed with professional internal auditors who adhere to the *Standards for the Professional Practice of Internal Auditing* and the related *Code of Ethics*. One of the best evidences of internal auditing competence is the Certified Internal Auditor (CIA) designation.

> Most internal auditors are degreed professionals. In fact, many hold advanced degrees and have acquired specialized skills related to the organization for which they work. These professionals are aware of their responsibilities with regard to the organization and the *Standards*.

The key proficiency of internal auditors is internal control in its broadest sense. Internal auditors provide management and the board of directors with competent evaluations of an organization's system of internal control and the quality of performance of assigned responsibilities regarding the reliability and integrity of information, compliance with laws and regulations, the safeguarding of assets, the economical and efficient use of resources, and accomplishment of goals and objectives.

Several common themes recur in control models such as the Committee of Sponsoring Organizations of the Treadway Commission, Criteria of Control Committee of the Canadian Institute of Chartered Accountants, and Cadbury Committee: "Internal Control is management's responsibility; tone from the top is important; controls must be built *in* not *on*; and internal communication and people development are critical elements of the control framework." Internal aduitors' value and effectiveness are linked not only to their attunement to management's philosophy and direction, but to their understanding of internal control and their direct knowledge of operating systems that are often in flux.

Internal auditors are in touch with governance issues and are intimately acquainted with their oganization's policies, procedures, operating practices, and personnel. They are able to devote their full attention and loyalty to the organization and to identify subtle changes and ambiguities that may signal trouble. Internal auditors can respond immediately to the concerns of senior management because they are familiar with their organizations' culture and processes, and their status as employees ensures confidentiality and loyalty.

As long as internal auditing staffs are highly skilled, efficient, and responsive to management, organizations are best served by keeping the internal auditing function internal.*

(e) Control Self-Assessment

Recently, in reaction to the ever-expanding requirements for internal audit services and the need to control overhead costs, internal audit groups have been turning to control self-assessment (CSA) reviews, also known as self-audits. CSA reviews are performed by line managers under the direction of the internal audit program. Most line managers are concerned about controls over their operations and have a basic knowledge of control issues related to their function or operation. Of course, CSA is not performed by individuals independent of the operations under review and, therefore, will only supplement, not replace internal audit activities.

In the current marketplace, all organizations are affected by global competition, as well as demands for greater accountability. Customer focused organizations are attempting to reengineer systems and eliminate activities that do not add value to customers. These programs are changing business processes very rapidly, and in some cases, reducing the internal control systems. At the same time, the profession of internal auditing, through The Institute of Internal Auditors and other professional associations including the AICPA and the Financial Executives Institute (FEI), have redefined internal control with a broader, more detailed definition, adding to the work of internal audit.

In this period of rapid change, CSA has arisen as a means of raising control awareness and coverage. This innovative approach provides the internal audit department with an opportunity to meet its audit customers (management) needs while controlling auditing costs.

CSA or self-auditing programs are usually built around self-audit questionnaires or audit programs. CSA programs are initiated by sending a letter about the program to line or operating managers explaining how the program will work, what their responsibilities will be (completion of the self-audit appraisal questionnaire) and how the information will be used by the internal audit

---

*From the IIA's Perspective on Internal Auditing, IIA-1994.

department. The letter should point out that the information will not only be reviewed, but will also be verified during subsequent audits.

A member of the audit department at the supervisor or manager level will review the CSA response and follow-up on noted significant control weaknesses immediately if deemed necessary. All less significant issues will be followed up at the point of the next audit. The CSA reports will also be integrated into the audit planning process. It is advisable to assign a supervisor or manager who is acquainted with the subject operations and/or who will be assigned to subsequent audits. Overtime, locations or operations subject to CSA reviews can be considered for extended audit intervals or lower risk assessments in the three-year plan. This will have the effect of reducing audit time and travel expenses. Of course, the quality of the CSA document and the seriousness with which local management implements the CSA program will be important factors.

CSA programs are relatively new methods of delivery of the internal audit service. Each organization will develop a program that fits with its organization. Another major benefit of this approach is that it allows the internal audit function to continue to evolve from the policing role to the facilitator of controls and policies role. Through CSA line or operations, managers assume more ownership and accountability for controls and participate in the process of reviewing and improving control effectiveness.

(f) Integrating the Auditing Process

The core process in an internal auditing function is the auditing process. This is supplemented by tangent processes such as personal development and quality assurance. The auditing process is defined in this manual as consisting of three major aspects:

1. The Planning Process

2. The Auditing Process

3. The Reporting Process.

We have learned that there exists the ability to link these processes and leverage work performed in one process to benefit the auditors, or reduce their work and thereby increase their productivity in a subsequent process. In addition, the methodology involves paying a great amount of attention to planning so that proper objectives are set and work is directed to the higher-risk areas within the organization. An example of the leverage is the use of information from the planning process including the scope and auditee profile in the resulting audit report. Good planning lends to improved effectiveness and better quality results.

This methodology has been successfully implemented in a number of audit departments, and although at first it may appear overly structured, the implementation has resulted in a consistently high-level, quality audit product. There are no government or professional requirements for internal audit management to be so structured; however, it has been my experience that operating in an unstructured environment causes; an erosion of management support and credibility over time.

Audit departments do not need to implement all of these strategies; however, they support the practice and provide management with a clear understanding of the process. Without this process, management may sometimes question the value or contribution of auditing.

1.2 CORPORATE AUDIT CHARTER

Audit departments should operate pursuant to a written charter indicating the purpose, authority, duties, and responsibilities of the function. The Audit Department Charter should be formally approved by the audit committee and the Board of Directors, updated periodically, and distributed to all company management.

The IIA Standards suggest the charter should (1) establish the department's position in the organization; (2) authorize access to records, locations, and personnel and (3) define the scope of internal activities. (See Figure 1.1.)

Figure 1.1   Sample Corporate Audit Charter*

(a)   Policy Statement

It is the policy of Sam Pole Company (the Corporation) to maintain an audit department as a means of providing the Board of Directors and all levels of management with information to assist in the control of operations and to assist senior management in reaching a conclusion concerning the overall control over assets and the effectiveness of the system of internal control in achieving its broad objectives. Additionally, the Audit Department will review the effectiveness and efficiency of operations and organizational structures.

Complementary objectives of the corporate audit department are to develop personnel. (See Personnel Administration and Recruiting, Chapter 5 and Marketing the Audit Function, Section 6.2.)

(b)   Responsibility of the Director of Auditing

The Director of Auditing is responsible for properly managing the department so that (1) audit work fulfills the purposes and responsibilities established herein; (2) resources are efficiently and effectively employed; and (3) audit work conforms to the Standards for the Professional Practice of Internal Auditing.

(c)   Reporting and Relationship to Audit Committee

The Director of Auditing will report to the Audit Committee for approval on audit scope, policy and administration. He will report in writing on all internal reviews conducted in the Corporation and will attend the committee meetings to report on significant recommendations and the operations of the internal audit function.

(d)   Independence

Independence is essential for effective operation of the internal audit function. It is the policy of the Corporation, therefore, that all audit activities shall remain free of influence by any organizational elements. This shall include such matters as scope of audit programs, the frequency and timing of examinations, and the content of audit reports.

*(Note: Adapted from *Guide to Accounting Controls*, Price Waterhouse, 1981, Warren, Gorham, Lamont.)

Figure 1.1 Continued

(e) Scope of Audit Activities

Audit coverage will encompass, as deemed appropriate by the Director of Auditing, independent reviews and evaluations of any and all management operations and activities to appraise:

- Measures taken to safeguard assets, including tests of existence and ownership as appropriate

- The reliability, consistency, and integrity of financial and operating information

- Compliance with policies, plans, standards, laws, and regulations that could have significant impact on operations

- Economy and efficiency in the use of resources

- Effectiveness in the accomplishment of the mission, objectives, and goals established for the Corporation's operations and projects.

Audit activities will be coordinated, to the extent possible, with the public accountants so as to enhance audit efficiency.

(f) Access and Confidentiality

In accomplishing his activities, the Director of Auditing and his staff are authorized to have full, free, and unrestricted access to all Corporation functions, activities, operations, records, data files, computer programs, property, and personnel. Under appropriate circumstances, the Director of Auditing is specifically authorized to communicate directly to the Chairman, President, and/or the Board of Directors. It is expected that the Director of Auditing and his staff will exercise discretion in the review of records to ensure the confidentiality of all matters that come to their attention.

(g) Responsibility for Corrective Action

The manager or head of the division, department, unit, or site audited is responsible for seeing that corrective action on recommendations made or deficient conditions reported by the auditor is either planned or taken. If the proper corrective action is not taken, the Director of Auditing is responsible for presenting a report on significant matters to a senior financial officer and/or the Audit Committee.

Figure 1.1   Continued

(h)   Limitation of Authority and Responsibility

In performing their functions, the Director of Auditing and corporate audit staff members have neither direct authority over, nor responsibility for, any of the activities reviewed. Internal auditors will not develop and install procedures, prepare records, make management decisions, or engage in any other activity which could be reasonably construed to compromise their independence. However, in connection with the complementary objectives of this audit function, Internal Audit will recommend accounting policies and procedures for approval and implementation by appropriate management. Therefore, internal audit review and appraisal do not in any way substitute for other activities or relieve other persons in the organization of the responsibilities assigned to them.

1.3 COMPANY ORGANIZATION

Auditors should be aware of their company structure and management organization. In order to provide this background, a section of this Manual should be devoted to a descripton of the company's activities. This can include a copy of the company's divisional or subsidiary organization structure. In addition to this structure, it is common to produce management organization charts. The senior management organization chart should be included in the internal audit manual. Figure 1.2, "Sam Pole Company Organization Chart," is an example of a high-level organization chart depicting the financial organization and the auditing organization.

The positioning of internal audit within a company can vary. There is a great debate in the profession that addresses the independence of internal auditing. The Sam Pole Company organization chart depicts the Director of Internal Auditing reporting directly to the Board of Directors, with a dotted-line responsibility to the Chief Financial Officer. In some companies, the internal auditing function reports directly to the Chief Financial Officer. This may be appropriate if the circumstances warrant this reporting relationship. Whenever possible, the reporting relationship should be independent of the financial organization.

Figure 1.2   Sam Pole Company Organization Chart

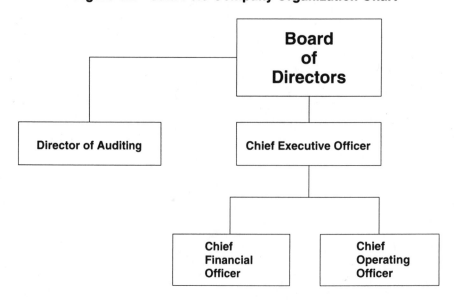

(a) Audit Department Organization

The Audit Department organization chart should be included in the Manual. If practical, it is beneficial to include the names of all the auditors in the department. This provides a level of personalization for the Manual. However, this approach will require more frequent revision.

Figure 1.3 is the Sam Pole Corporate Audit Department organization chart. The chart depicts an integrated audit department approach in which staff are available to managers of each audit discipline. This is an unusual approach and was included in this version of the manual to provide a

Figure 1.3   Sam Pole Corporate Audit Department Organization Chart

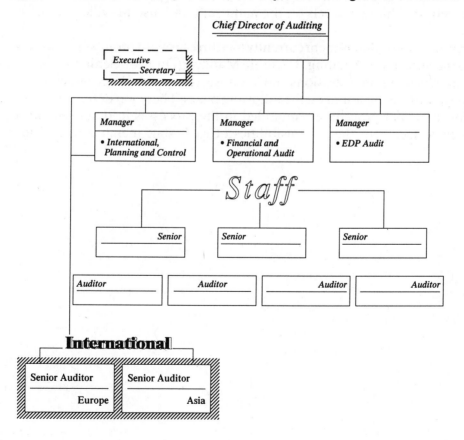

SAM POLE COMPANY	(LOGO)	CORPORATE AUDIT DEPARTMENT	
		PROCEDURES MANUAL	DATE:

TITLE: Company Organization	NO: 1.3	PAGES:

thought-provoking example. Most departments have organization charts which can be easily included in this section of the manual. The Job Classifications/Descriptions that follow have been developed in a format consistent with this organization chart.

Another method for improving commitment and team spirit is to include the names of all the department members on a departmental routing slip. This routing slip can augment the organization chart.

(b)   Job Classifications and Descriptions

Job descriptions formally define the functions, duties, and responsibilities of a position. They also indicate the knowledge and skills required for successful performance. As such, they provide a vehicle for defining different levels on the audit staff and also provide criteria for performance evaluation.

The Corporate Audit Department currently has three levels of professional job classifications, in addition to the Director of Auditing. These are Manager/Director, Senior Auditor and Auditor. In addition, there is one nonprofessional position: secretary. Job descriptions for the current professional positions can be found on the following pages. These job descriptions reference responsibilities for the major procedures contained in the processes in other sections of the manual. Therefore, they document the responsibilities of each staff member related to these methodologies.

POSITION NAME: DIRECTOR OF AUDITING

REPORTS TO: Senior Officer for Administration and the Board of Directors (usually through the Audit Committee) for audit scope and policy.

FUNCTION: The position is responsible for properly managing the department so that (1) audit work fulfills the purposes and responsibilities established in the department charter; (2) resources are efficiently and effectively employed; and (3) audit work conforms to the Standards for the Professional Practice of Internal Auditing.

DUTIES AND RESPONSIBILITIES:

To direct independent reviews and evaluations of any and all management operations and activities to appraise:

- The reliability and integrity of financial and operating information

- Compliance with policies, plans, standards, laws, and regulations that could have significant impact upon operations

- Measures taken to safeguard assets, including tests of existence and ownership as appropriate

- Economy and efficiency in the use of resources

- Effectiveness in the accomplishment of objectives and goals established for corporation operations and projects.

To coordinate activities to the extent possible with the public accountants to enhance audit efficiency.

To exercise discretion in the review of records to ensure confidentiality.

To present to a senior officer and/or the Audit Committee, a report on significant recommendations or deficiencies on which audited management has not taken proper corrective action.

To ensure that the department does not develop or install procedures, prepare records, make management decisions, or engage in any other activity that could be reasonably construed to compromise its independence.

The Director must have an in-depth knowledge of the audit profession as well as the audit function at Sam Pole Company, from both conceptual and technical viewpoints. Therefore, the Director should maintain an expert knowledge of the auditing profession.

The Director must have excellent written and verbal communication skills as well as excellent editing skills. He/she is responsible for monthly activity reports to senior management and updates to the Corporate Audit Procedures Manual. The Director will perform a final review of corporate audit reports.

The Director should have excellent interpersonal skills. These skills are critical to develop and maintain effective working relationships with all levels of management, the external auditors, consultants, and various industry representatives.

The Director will also need to counsel managers and audit staff members as to their performance and career development.

International:

Sam Pole Company is a dynamic company with significant operations all over the world. The Audit Director will be involved with audits in foreign and domestic locations. This will involve travel to foreign and domestic locations, where in some cases English may not be the first language.

CONTACTS—INTERNAL AND EXTERNAL:

Internally, the incumbent deals directly with all levels of management in the company. The incumbent works with the corporate audit staff, managers and senior officers of the company.

Externally, the incumbent maintains close relationships with the Institute of Internal Auditors (IIA) and the American Institute of Certified Public Accountants (AICPA) in order to keep abreast of trends and developments in the auditing profession. He/she has regular dealings with managers and partners of the company's external auditors to obtain material including information that should be disseminated to the audit staff and management of the company.

He/she develops contacts with suppliers of materials and other supplies for the functioning of the Audit Department.

QUALIFICATIONS—MINIMUM KNOWLEDGE AND SKILLS:

This individual will have at least a four-year college degree and approximately ten to fifteen years of experience in Internal Auditing and External Auditing, including at least seven years at the manager or director level

- A CPA or CIA certification
- Experience with financial, operational, and management auditing
- Experience in a manufacturing and/or distribution environment
- A good general understanding of EDP Auditing
- The ideal candidate will also possess foreign language skills.

POSITION NAME: AUDIT MANAGER—
INTERNATIONAL, PLANNING AND CONTROL

REPORTS TO: Director of Auditing

FUNCTION: This position is responsible for overall audit planning, policies and procedures, coordination with external audit and consultants, and quality assurance.

The position is responsible for insuring that the overall audit function of the company monitors trends in the auditing field and applies them when appropriate to the practice of auditing in the company. The position is also responsible for coordinating/initiating all planning, quality assurance and human resources-related functions for the Corporate Audit Department. Furthermore, the position is responsible for the preparation and implementation of a training plan for the department and the individual professionals therein and coordinating the activities of internationally-based auditors.

DUTIES AND RESPONSIBILITIES:

The individual will have direct responsibility for preparing an Audit Department multi-year plan, and:

- Coordinates input from the Director of Auditing as well as audit managers in developing the plan

- Summarizes input received from managers and Director of Auditing, with international plans, and produces a draft plan for discussion

- Updates drafts based on input received until final draft is approved

- Prepares six-month and one-year plans from the three-year plan.

The individual will be responsible for the coordination and administration of the Audit Department; and:

- Develop and maintain the Audit Procedures Manual of the Corporate Audit Department

- Prepare the operating budget for the department for approval by the Director of Auditing

- Monitor expenses by overseeing purchases and payment of invoices, and recommending viable alternatives to the audit management

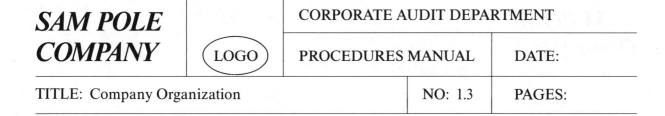
- Prepare annual summaries of external audit fees for the Director of Auditing

- Prepare periodic reports for senior management for the Director of Auditing's review; also oversee the preparation and production of periodic and biannual audit report summaries to the Audit Committee

- Maintain a complete file on each member of the audit staff, which contains job descriptions, resumes, career actions, performance appraisals, training plans and development records; produces and analyzes reports on various personnel statistics

- Advise Corporate Audit management on training needs and availability.

The individual will be responsible for developing and implementing the department's Quality Assurance Program; and:

- Maintain the department's policies regarding periodic reviews of entire assignments, summary reviews of all assignments, and external peer review

- Schedule staff for reviews of entire engagements

- Schedule staff for summary reviews of each engagement on an availability basis

- Prepare reports for the Director of Auditing, discussing the areas where improvement is needed in the audit process.

Internationally Based Auditors:

The individual will be responsible for coordinating the activities of the internationally based auditors:

- To coordinate the development of the international audit plans and integrate them into domestic plans

- To monitor the activities of the internationally based auditors

- To provide guidance on company developments.

Audits:

In addition to the significant administrative responsibilities discussed in the job description, the individual will be involved in selected audits, both domestic and international.

This position is responsible for maintaining expert knowledge of the auditing profession. The incumbent must keep abreast of new or proposed developments to the auditing function, and analyze their impact on the company. In addition, the incumbent is an authoritative source of information to the audit group as regards the practice of auditing.

- The incumbent must have an in-depth knowledge of the audit profession as well as the audit function at Sam Pole Company, from both conceptual and technical viewpoints. Also the incumbent should have a good understanding of the company's primary lines of business and organizational structure—or if such knowledge is minimal, should be capable of quickly becoming familiar with these activities.

- The incumbent must have excellent written and verbal communications skills as well as excellent editing skills. In addition, the incumbent must prepare monthly activity reports to senior management and update (as necessary) the Corporate Audit Procedures Manual. The manager must review and edit corporate audit reports and be able to effectively communicate departmental policies and procedures to staff.

- Well-developed interpersonal skills are critical to develop and maintain effective working relationships with all levels of in-house management, the company's external auditors and consultants, and various industry representatives. The incumbent also needs to counsel audit staff members as to selected training and career development.

- Develop and maintain ongoing contact with peers in industry for the purpose of gathering information and exchanging ideas.

- Gather information on proposed legislation, analyze impact to the company, and draft statements for the Director of Auditing's consideration.

- Interact with associations and institutions to keep abreast of developments and trends in the auditing profession and insure that both the Audit Department and business units are kept informed.

International:

Sam Pole Company is a dynamic company with significant operations all over the world. Audit managers and staff will be involved with audits in foreign and domestic locations. This will involve travel, for periods of time, to foreign and domestic locations where, in some cases, English may not be the first language.

CONTACTS—INTERNAL AND EXTERNAL:

Internally, the incumbent deals directly with all levels of management in the audit function of the company, in order to provide guidance when requested. The incumbent works with the Corporate Audit staff and senior officers of the company including cross-relationships with Human Resources, Officer Services, and Information Systems.

Externally, the incumbent maintains close relationships with the Institute of Internal Auditors (IIA) and the American Institute of Certified Public Accountants (AICPA) in order to keep abreast of trends and developments in the auditing profession. He/she has regular dealings with managers and partners of the company's external auditors to obtain material including information that should be disseminated to the audit staff and management of the company.

He/she develops contacts with suppliers of materials and other supplies for the functioning of the Audit Department.

QUALIFICATIONS—MINIMUM KNOWLEDGE AND SKILLS:

This individual will have a four-year college degree and possess approximately five to eight years experience in Internal Auditing.

- The ideal candidate will also possess foreign language skills.
- A CPA or CIA is desirable.

POSITION NAME: AUDIT MANAGER—FINANCIAL/OPERATIONAL AUDIT

REPORTS TO: Director of Auditing

FUNCTION: Responsible for properly managing the department so that (1) audit work fulfills the purposes and responsibilities established in the department; (2) resources are efficiently and effectively employed; and (3) audit work conforms to the Standards for the Professional Practice of Internal Auditing, published by the Institute of Internal Auditors and the General Standards for Information Systems Auditing published by The IS Auditor and Control Foundation.

DUTIES AND RESPONSIBILITIES:

To direct independent reviews and evaluations of any and all management operations and activities to appraise:

- Reliability and integrity of financial and operating information

- Compliance with policies, plans, standards, laws, and regulations which could have significant impact upon operations

- Effectiveness in accomplishment of objectives and goals established for the corporation and projects

- Measures taken to safeguard assets, including tests of existence and ownership as appropriate

- Economy, effectiveness, and efficiency in use of resources (operational audits)

- Effectiveness of organizational structures to achieve corporate goals and ability of Management to plan, organize, direct, and control its function (Management Auditing).

To coordinate activities to the extent possible with the public accountants to enhance audit efficiency.

To exercise discretion in the review of records to ensure confidentiality of all matters that come to attention.

For All Assigned Audits:

- Implement the Department procedures for audit planning, establishing scope, and determining appropriate audit procedures

- Develop or review the following audit documents on audits assigned:

  - Preliminary survey: Review planned survey; review survey results
  - Audit time budget
  - Planning memo
  - Audit programs.

- Preaudit conference: Establish audit objectives to be discussed at conference

- Field work: Perform or review field work, as appropriate

- Workpapers: Perform a limited review, as appropriate, based on senior detail review of workpapers. Approve reviewed workpapers for filing

- Interim recommendations following field work and documentation of auditee position

- Status memo: the basis of memo contents, consider appropriateness of original audit plan and scope or need to modify to attain audit objective

- Closing conference: Plan and conduct audit closing conference

- Report Preparation/Review: Develop, review, and approve revisions before submitting reports to the Director of Auditing and Audit Committee

- Summary Memo: Review results of audit regarding attainment of objectives. Review and approve comparison of actual with budgeted hours and explanation for variance

- Audit Management Letter: Review and follow-up on all profit center responses to the public accountants' Audit Management Letter, including a report to the Audit Committee

- Performance Evaluation: Prepare evaluation of senior auditors and conduct review

- Information Systems: Have sufficient basic EDP knowledge to be able to discuss and determine application of EDP audit resources

- Decision making responsibility, conclusions: Responsible for administrative and audit related decision making and conclusions based upon completed audits

- Counsel/Guide/Motivate: Provide direction to immediate assistants to enable them to counsel, guide, and motivate staff. Participates directly in this activity when appropriate

- Auditee Relationship: At executive management level, identify and develop audit opportunities to provide a more effective audit service to management.

Other Matters:

- Special investigations: Provide direction and guidance. Review results. Recommend action in coordination with other interested company and outside parties

- Continuing Education: Pursue regular program for continuing education for self, (related to certification). Review and approve suitable program for department staff

- Special Projects: As assigned, may participate. Direct, review, evaluate, and report work of assistants

- Professionalism: Demonstrate superior performance and direction in all attributes of professional conduct of self and staff.

International:

Sam Pole is a dynamic company with significant operations all over the world. Audit managers and staff will be involved with audits in foreign and domestic locations. This will involve travel to foreign locations where in some cases English may not be the first language.

CONTACTS—INTERNAL AND EXTERNAL:

Internally, the incumbent deals directly with all levels of management in the audit function of the company, in order to provide guidance when requested. The incumbent works with the Corporate Audit staff and senior officers of the company especially with the accounting functions.

Externally, the incumbent maintains close relationships with the Institute of Internal Auditors (IIA) and the American Institute of Certified Public Accountants (AICPA), if applicable, in order to keep abreast of trends and developments in the auditing profession. The incumbent has regular dealings with managers and partners of the company's external auditors to obtain material including information that should be disseminated to the audit staff and management of the company. Contact with organizations specializing in operational and management auditing must be maintained.

QUALIFICATIONS—MINIMUM KNOWLEDGE AND SKILLS:

- A degree in accounting or other qualified discipline
- CPA or CIA
- Experience in a manufacturing and/or distribution environment
- Experience in a supervisory capacity and the ability to direct and develop others
- Experience with Financial, Operational, and Management Auditing.

POSITION NAME: AUDIT MANAGER—EDP AUDIT

REPORTS TO: Director of Auditing

FUNCTION: Responsible for properly managing the department so that (1) audit work fulfills the purposes and responsibilities established in the department (2) resources are efficiently and effectively employed; and (3) audit work conforms to the Standards for the Professional Practice of Internal Auditing, published by the IIA, and the General Standards for Information Systems Auditing published by The IS Audit and Control Foundation.

DUTIES AND RESPONSIBILITIES:

The individual will have primary responsibility for reviews of the company's Information Systems environment:

To direct independent reviews and evaluations of any and all management operations and activities to appraise:

- Reliability and integrity of information systems (IS)

- Compliance with policies, plans, standards, laws, and regulations which could have significant impact upon IS systems or operations

- Effectiveness in accomplishment of objectives and goals of IS

- Measures taken by IS to safeguard assets, including tests of existence and ownership as appropriate

- Economy and efficiency in use of IS resources

- Involvement in Systems Development audits to insure controls are built in during the systems development life cycle (SDLC) process.

To develop an audit program to address systems in development including:

- Analyses of SDLC methodology, providing for internal audit input at key points in the process

- Planning of audits of development projects (or ongoing audit involvements) to provide critical input while the project is in process.

The individual will be responsible for taking a leadership position in expanding the use of computers by the audit staff:

- Expanding use of computer-assisted audit techniques (CAATs) to support audit projects

- Monitor the department's data processing requirements for micro-tools including audit software and administrative packages

- Establish and maintain an automated time and expenses reporting system.

The position is responsible for maintaining an expert knowledge of the EDP Auditing profession. The individual must keep abreast of new and proposed developments in the EDP Auditing field and analyze the impact on the company. He/she should be an authoritative source of information to the audit group as regards the practice of auditing.

- The incumbent must have a good working knowledge of the Information Systems developments at Sam Pole Company. Consideration should be given to attending IS Steering Committee meetings

- The incumbent must have excellent written and verbal communication skills as well as excellent editing skills. He/she must prepare monthly activity reports to senior management on EDP Auditing activities.

To coordinate activities to the extent possible with the public accountants to enhance audit efficiency.

To exercise discretion in the review of records to ensure confidentiality of all matters that come to attention.

The position will be responsible for working on selected financial and operational audits. These will supplement the primary area of responsibility of EDP Auditing.

For All Assigned Audits:

- Implement the Department procedures for audit planning, establishing scope, and determining appropriate audit procedures

- Develop or review the following audit documents on audits assigned:
  - Preliminary survey: Review planned survey; review survey results
  - Audit time budget

SAM POLE COMPANY (LOGO)

CORPORATE AUDIT DEPARTMENT

PROCEDURES MANUAL

DATE:

TITLE: Company Organization

NO: 1.3

PAGES:

- Planning memo
- Audit programs

- Preaudit conference: Establish audit objectives to be discussed at conference

- Field work: Perform or review field work, as appropriate

- Workpapers: Perform a limited review, as appropriate, based on senior detail review of workpapers. Approve reviewed workpapers for filing

- Interim recommendations following field work and documentation of auditee position

- Status memo: the basis of memo contents, consider appropriateness of original audit plan and scope or need to modify to attain audit objective

- Closing conference: Plan and conduct audit closing conference

- Report Preparation/Review: Develop, review, and approve revisions before submitting reports to the Director of Auditing and Audit Committee

- Summary Memo: Review results of audit regarding attainment of objectives. Review and approve comparison of actual with budgeted hours and explanation for variance

- Audit Management Letter: Review and follow-up on all responses to the public accountants' Audit Management Letter, including a report to the Audit Committee

- Performance Evaluation: Prepare evaluation of senior auditor and conduct review

- Decision making responsibility, conclusions: Responsible for administrative and audit related decision making and conclusions based upon completed audits

- Counsel/Guide/Motivate: Provide direction to immediate assistants to enable them to counsel, guide and motivate staff. Participate directly in this activity when appropriate

- Auditee Relationship: At executive management level, identify and develop audit opportunities to provide a more effective audit service to management.

Other Matters:

- Special investigations: Provide direction and guidance. Review results. Recommend action in coordination with other interested company and outside parties

- Continuing Education: Pursue regular program for continuing education for self, (related to certification). Review and approve suitable program for department staff

- Special Projects: As assigned, may participate. Direct, review, evaluate, and report work of assistants

- Professionalism: Demonstrate superior performance and direction in all attributes of professional conduct of self and staff.

International:

Sam Pole is a dynamic company with significant operations all over the world. Audit managers and staff will be involved with audits in foreign and domestic locations. This will involve travel, for periods of time, to foreign locations, where, in some cases, English may not be the first language.

CONTACTS—INTERNAL AND EXTERNAL:

Internally, the incumbent deals directly with all levels of management in the audit function of the company, in order to provide guidance when requested. The incumbent works with the Corporate Audit staff and senior officers of the company especially with Information Systems.

Externally, the incumbent maintains a close relationship with The EDP Auditors Association (EDPAA) in order to keep abreast of trends and developments in the EDP Auditing profession. He/she has regular dealings with managers and partners of the company's external auditors to obtain material including information that should be disseminated to the audit staff and management of the company. He/she maintains contact with audit software vendors to stay abreast of developments in the field.

QUALIFICATIONS—MINIMUM KNOWLEDGE AND SKILLS:

The individual will have a college degree and possess approximately six to ten years of experience in Internal Auditing and EDP Auditing.

- A four-year degree with a major in accounting and/or data processing

- A Certified Information Systems Auditor designation

- Experience in a manufacturing and/or distribution environment

- Experience with IBM mainframe and mid-range computer systems

- Experience in a supervisory capacity

- CPA or CIA (not essential).

POSITION NAME: SENIOR AUDITOR

REPORTS TO: Internal Audit Manager

FUNCTION: Plan, organize, conduct, supervise, and formally report on a scheduled audit.

DUTIES AND RESPONSIBILITIES:

- Planning Scope and Procedures: Develop or supervise assistants in planning the scope for audits and selection and development of appropriate audit procedures for manager approval

- Preliminary Survey: Direct the development and preparation of the survey approach. Participate and oversee work by assistants, if applicable

- Audit Time Budget: Ensure establishing a practical budget, completing work on time and evaluating performance and variance

- Planning Memo: Review assistant input and document thorough and complete approved plan for specific audits after obtaining general guidelines from manager

- Audit Programs-Development/changes: With manager approval, develop audit programs necessary to promote effective audit coverage

- Pre-audit Conference: Ensure that audit objectives have been clearly and completely set forth to the auditee before the audit

- Field Work: Perform all field work in a competent and professional manner. Provide evidential support for all report recommendations

- Identifying System Control Points: Document controls or perform expert review of work by assistants

- Workpapers: Prepare selected workpapers and review assistants' workpapers

- Interim Recommendations: Prepare recommendations for auditee consideration; review and evaluate assistants' recommendations, considering materiality, pertinence to audit and documentary evidence

- Status Memo: Prepare or review draft and finalize status memo for presentation to manager

- Closing Conference: Prepare or review agenda of recommendations and comments. Conduct with support from assistants

- Report Preparation/Review: Prepare or review detailed recommendations and comments for materiality and relativity of items, adequacy of workpaper documentation and auditee position (if known). Responsible for completeness and accuracy of entire report subject to manager approval

- Summary Memo: Prepare or review final summary memo based on review and evaluation of input by assistants. Submit future audit planning recommendations

- Performance Evaluation: Complete timely performance evaluations for assistant on audit and reviews evaluations with them (if applicable)

- EDP: Apply, in appropriate circumstances, knowledge of basic EDP audit techniques

- Procedures-Audit/Company: Demonstrate complete comprehension and ability to (1) assess validity of existing policies and procedures and (2) recommend sound alternatives

- Decision making responsibility, conclusions: Demonstrate capacity and evidence for effective decision making and drawing sound conclusions

- Auditee Relationships: Ensure continuing development of effective professional relationships with auditee personnel

- Special Investigations: Possess ability to carry out assignments discreetly, effectively, and efficiently in sensitive, confidential circumstances

- Awareness of the State-of-the-Art: Demonstrate clear understanding of current developments, associating that understanding with company audit applications. Recommend adaptation, where appropriate, in our audit approach

- Continuing Education: Pursue departmental approved program for continuing education for self and recommend suitable programs for department associates

- Travel: Meet requirements and recommend improvements and alternatives to ensure timely, effective realization of department audit plan

- Special Projects: Participate, as assigned. Recommend special projects, based upon experience and/or need

- Professionalism: Demonstrate superior performance in all attributes of professional conduct. Encourage others towards comparable performance.

International:

Sam Pole is a dynamic company with significant operations all over the world. Audit managers and staff will be involved with audits in foreign and domestic locations. This will involve travel, for periods of time, to foreign locations, where, in some cases, English may not be the first language.

CONTACTS—INTERNAL AND EXTERNAL:

Internally, department management and associates; most levels of auditee management. Externally, technical and other business professionals through societies and association memberships.

QUALIFICATIONS (MINIMUM KNOWLEDGE AND SKILLS)

- Have achieved or work towards certification by examination
- Have undergraduate degree in accounting (or qualified discipline)
- Have achieved high academic standing
- Have ability to supervise and work well with people
- Have special skills or knowledge and the ability to instruct, train, and develop others in those skills
- Have apparent management potential.

SAM POLE COMPANY	(LOGO)	CORPORATE AUDIT DEPARTMENT	
		PROCEDURES MANUAL	DATE:

TITLE: Company Organization	NO: 1.3	PAGES:

POSITION NAME: AUDITOR

REPORTS TO: Senior Auditor

FUNCTION: Plan, organize, conduct, and formally report on a scheduled audit.

DUTIES AND RESPONSIBILITIES:

- Planning Scope and Procedures: Develop the scope for audits and selection and development of appropriate audit procedures for senior/manager approval

- Preliminary Survey: Development and preparation of the survey

- Audit Time Budget: Ensure establishing a practical budget, completing work on time, and evaluating performance and variance

- Planning Memo: Provide input and document plan for specific audits after obtaining general guidelines from senior/manager

- Audit Programs-Development/changes: With senior approval, develop audit programs necessary to promote effective audit coverage

- Pre-audit Conference: Ensure that audit objectives have been clearly and completely set forth to the auditee before the audit

- Field Work: Perform all field work in a competent and professional manner. Provide evidential support for all report recommendations

- Identifying System Control Points: Document controls

- Workpapers: Prepare selected workpapers

- Interim Recommendations: Prepare recommendations for auditee consideration; review, considering materiality, pertinence to audit and documentary evidence

- Status Memo: Prepare draft status memo for presentation to manager

- Closing Conference: Prepare preliminary agenda of recommendations and comments

- Report Preparation/Review: Prepare detailed recommendations and comments

- Summary Memo: Prepare preliminary summary memo. Submit future audit planning recommendations

- Performance Evaluation: Complete timely performance evaluations for assistant on audit and reviews evaluations with them (if applicable)

- EDP: Apply, in appropriate circumstances, knowledge of basic EDP audit techniques

- Procedures-Audit/Company: Demonstrate complete comprehension and ability to (1) assess validity of existing policies and procedures and (2) recommend sound alternatives

- Decision making responsibility, conclusions: Demonstrate capacity and evidence for effective decision making and drawing sound conclusions

- Auditee Relationships: Ensure continuing development of effective professional relationships with auditee personnel

- Special Investigations: Possess ability to carry out assignments discreetly, effectively, and efficiently in sensitive, confidential circumstances

- Awareness of the State-of-the-Art: Demonstrate basic understanding of current developments, associating that understanding with company audit applications. Recommend adaptation, where appropriate, in our audit approach

- Continuing Education: Pursue departmental approved program for continuing education for self

- Travel: Meet requirements and recommend improvements and alternatives to ensure timely, effective realization of department audit plan

- Special Projects: Participate, as assigned. Recommend special projects, based upon experience and/or need

- Professionalism: Demonstrate superior performance in all attributes of professional conduct. Encourage others towards comparable performance.

International:

Sam Pole is a dynamic company with significant operations all over the world. Audit managers and staff will be involved with audits in foreign and domestic locations. This will involve some travel to foreign locations where in some cases English may not be the first language.

CONTACTS—INTERNAL AND EXTERNAL:

Internally, department management and associates; most levels of auditee management. Externally, technical and other business professionals through societies and association memberships.

QUALIFICATIONS (MINIMUM KNOWLEDGE AND SKILLS):

- Have achieved or work towards certification by examination
- Have undergraduate degree in accounting (or qualified discipline)
- Have achieved high academic standing
- Have ability to supervise and gets along with people
- Have special skills or knowledge and the ability to instruct, train, and develop others in those skills
- Have apparent management potential.

POSITION NAME: SENIOR AUDITOR—EUROPE [INTERNATIONAL LOCATION]

REPORTS TO: Audit Manager—Planning and Control

FUNCTION: This position is responsible for performing audits in Sam Pole's European operations. Corporate audit procedures established in the US, to the extent possible, will be followed by the Senior Auditor—Europe.

DUTIES AND RESPONSIBILITIES:

The individual will have direct responsibility for preparing preliminary, annual, and multi-year audit plans for approval in the United States, for all European operations.

The individual will prepare drafts of expense budgets for one-year plans as appropriate, for approval in the United States. The individual will maintain a copy of the Corporate Audit Policies & Procedures Manual of the Corporate Audit Department for use in Europe.

The individual will maintain contact and develop lines of communication with auditees throughout the European operations.

The individual will attempt to maintain a knowledge of developments in the various European operations. This will involve monitoring periodic management reports and staying apprised of economic developments in each country. Periodically, reports on these developments will be made to the Manager—Planning and Control.

For All Assigned Audits:

- Planning Scope and Procedures: Develop or supervise assistants in planning the scope for audits and selection and development of appropriate audit procedures for manager approval

- Preliminary Survey: Direct the development and preparation of the survey approach. Participate and oversee work by assistants, if applicable

- Audit Time Budget: Ensure establishing a practical budget, completing work on time and evaluating performance and variance

- Planning Memo: Review assistant input and document a thorough and completely approved plan for specific audits after obtaining general guidelines from manager

- Audit Programs-Development/changes: With manager approval, develop audit programs necessary to promote effective audit coverage

- Pre-audit Conference: Ensure that audit objectives have been clearly and completely set forth to the auditee before the audit

- Field Work: Perform all field work in a competent and professional manner. Provide evidential support for all report recommendations

- Identifying System Control Points: Perform expert review of work by assistants

- Workpapers: Prepare selected workpapers and review assistants' workpapers

- Interim Recommendations: Prepare recommendations for auditee consideration; review and evaluate assistants' recommendations, considering materiality, pertinence to audit and documentary evidence

- Status Memo: Prepare or review draft and finalize status memo for presentation to manager

- Closing Conference: Prepare or review agenda of recommendations and comments. Conduct with support from assistants

- Report Preparation/Review: Prepare or review detailed recommendations and comments for materiality and relativity of items, adequacy of workpaper documentation and auditee position (if known). Responsible for completeness and accuracy of entire report subject to manager approval

- Summary Memo: Prepare or review final summary memo based on review and evaluation of input by assistants. Submit future audit planning recommendations

- Performance Evaluation: Complete timely performance evaluations for assistant on audit and reviews evaluations with them, if applicable

- EDP: Apply, in appropriate circumstances, knowledge of basic EDP audit techniques

- Procedures-Audit/Company: Demonstrate complete comprehension and ability to (1) assess validity of existing policies and procedures and (2) recommend sound alternatives

- Decision making responsibility, conclusions: Demonstrate capacity and evidence for effective decision making and drawing sound conclusions

- Auditee Relationships: Ensure continuing development of effective professional relationships with auditee personnel

- Special Investigations: Possess ability to carry out assignments discreetly, effectively and efficiently in sensitive, confidential circumstances

- Awareness of the State-of-the-Art: Demonstrate clear understanding of current developments, associating that understanding with company audit applications. Recommend adaptation, where appropriate, in our audit approach

- Continuing Education: Pursue departmental approved program for continuing education for self and recommends suitable programs for department associates

- Travel: Meet requirements and recommend improvements and alternatives to ensure timely, effective realization of department audit plan

- Special Projects: Participate, as assigned. Recommend special projects, based upon experience and/or need

- Professionalism: Demonstrate superior performance in all attributes of professional conduct. Encourages others toward comparable performance.

International:

Sam Pole is a dynamic company with headquarters in the United States and significant operations all over the world. All audit managers and staff are involved with audits in foreign and domestic locations. This involves some travel to foreign locations, where, in some cases, language differences may be encountered. The Senior Auditor—Europe will possess multilanguage skills and/or recommend alternative audit approaches including use of outside accountants or other company personnel.

CONTACTS—INTERNAL AND EXTERNAL:

Internally, the incumbent deals directly with all levels of management in the European headquarters and country operations. Requests for audit assistance by the operating units should be communicated to United States headquarters and considered during the planning process. The position works closely with the Director of Finance for European Operations.

Externally, the incumbent should be a member of the Institute of Internal Auditors (UK) and other appropriate audit institutes in Europe. The incumbent will have regular dealings with managers and partners of the company's external auditors.

SAM POLE COMPANY   (LOGO)

CORPORATE AUDIT DEPARTMENT		
PROCEDURES MANUAL	DATE:	
TITLE: Company Organization	NO: 1.3	PAGES:

QUALIFICATIONS—MINIMUM KNOWLEDGE AND SKILLS:

- Have achieved or work towards certification by examination

- Have undergraduate degree in accounting, (or qualified discipline). (Having achieved high academic standing, i.e., honors)

- Have fluent command of English and other language skills

- Have experience in the multinational auditing environment

- Have ability to supervise and get along with people

- Have experience in the distribution or direct-sell business

- Have special skills or knowledge and the ability to instruct, train, and develop others in those skills

- Have apparent management potential

- Independent thinker.

1.4 CORPORATE AUDIT POLICIES

In addition to the specific department procedures and administrative programs (contained in Chapter 5), the department should have various policies. The examples of these policies include the ones included in this chapter. However, these should not be considered all inclusive by any means. All departments should have a confidentiality policy and travel and entertainment policies. These would be the minimum policies, and every effort should be made to document policies on a case-by-case basis as they arise. This section can be used as the area to record all department policies.

Confidentiality

Orientation

Days Off for Extensive Travel

Professional Certification Policy

(a) Confidentiality

(i) Background

In accordance with the approved Corporate Audit Department Charter under subsection Access and Confidentiality, "in accomplishing his activities, the Director of Auditing and his staff are authorized to have full, free, and unrestricted access to all corporation functions, activities, operations, records, data files, computer programs, property and personnel."

This exposes the staff to confidential corporate information either by examination or discussion. The privileged permission to be informed of confidential information carries a responsibility for the audit department staff's confidentiality.

Confidentiality is defined as to "hold secret." The only exception is to report to audit management and others on a defensible need-to-know basis.

(ii) Policy

All information known to require or deemed to (by a reasonable person test) require confidentiality should be kept so.

(iii) Discussion

Corporate Audit Department management is forced to guard their responsibility for staff confidentiality to protect the department's reputation and credibility. This includes present staff, transfers, and past employees.

Breaches of confidentiality may be either intentional or by accident, as being overheard in public places, elevators, or restaurants.

We are involved in and knowledgeable in a number of sensitive company situations including union agreements, company politics, different pay scales, and special investigations that require good judgment and limited exposure of details.

Another area of which the auditor must be constantly aware is gossip. Many people on the company grapevine feel creditability is given to their conversation if they can include "I heard it from an auditor." So be aware of the person who asks a lot of questions.

It should be clear to current or past employees of the Corporate Audit Department violations of confidentiality or gossip may result in:

- Immediate termination
- Probation
- Suspension without pay

- Warning

- Lawsuit.

The consequences will be at the judgment of the Director of Auditing and/or Audit Committee. A lawsuit could result from third party damage as defamation of character from a libelous or slanderous statement. (See section on Responsibilities of an Auditor.)

(b) Orientation (Training)

(i) Objective
Provide reasonable assurance that the new employee will become promptly productive.

(ii) Responsibility
Orientation is the responsibility of the manager to whom the new employee reports.

(iii) Orientation Outline (see Section 5.6)

- Information about Sam Pole Company
- Information about the Internal Audit Department at the Company
- Introduction to audit staff personnel and other employees with whom the auditor will work
- Discussion of duties and responsibilities
- Control of work:
  - Hours of work
  - Time reports
  - Paycheck distribution
  - Travel regulations
  - Expense report preparation
  - Supplies
- Readings:
  - Audit manual
  - Standards
  - Literature on modern internal auditing
  - Recent audit reports.

(See Recommended Reading List)

SAM POLE COMPANY (LOGO)

CORPORATE AUDIT DEPARTMENT

PROCEDURES MANUAL

DATE:

TITLE: Corporate Audit Policies

NO: 1.4

PAGES:

(c) Days Off for Extensive Travel Policy

No specific corporate policy has been set forth on this subject. Therefore, the following policy for the Internal Audit Department will apply:

- One day for each seven consecutive nights in an international location may be taken off with pay

- One day for the first 14 consecutive days of domestic (North American) travel may be taken off with pay. For every additional seven consecutive and contiguous days thereafter, one additional day off may be taken

- Such days must be utilized by the end of the calendar year or they are automatically forfeited.

(d) Professional Certification Policy

In order to encourage professional development within the Corporate Audit Department at Sam Pole Company, the Company will support employees who wish to attain a recognized professional recognition through certification. The programs currently being supported include the Certified Internal Auditor (CIA), the Certified Information Systems Auditor (CISA), the Certified Public Accountant (CPA), and the Certified Management Accountant (CMA). The successful completion of these written examinations will result in a demonstration of personal achievement and enhance the professional posture for the department.

In order to encourage employees to attain professional recognition by passing an exam certification, the Company will assist staff members by providing:

1. The cost of registration and fees for the initial sitting for the examination

2. Fifty percent of the cost for recognized preparation (review) courses to a maximum of $500. To avoid misunderstanding, selected courses should be approved by the Director of Auditing prior to registration and payment of fees. Attendance at classes is to be scheduled during non-working hours (Monday through Friday) or, preferably, on weekends.

    Staff assignments to projects will consider review course attendance, but Sam Pole work must take precedence in cases where staff members are required to fulfill Company commitments;

3. Time for sitting for examinations will be considered authorized excused leave.

It is anticipated that the Company will benefit from the attainment of certifications through increased professional knowledge and adherence to professional standards and codes of conduct.

1.5 STANDARDS FOR THE PROFESSIONAL PRACTICE OF INTERNAL AUDITING

(a) Adoption of the Standards

In June 1978, the Institute of Internal Auditors, Board of Directors, formally adopted a set of standards for internal auditors. These Standards apply to all internal auditors and are incorporated in this Manual by reference.

Internal auditors around the world have been practicing their craft in different ways. Most have been functioning under the direction of the people to whom they report, running the gamut from chief accountants to CEOs.

Certainly, no set of standards can dictate management's disposition of its internal auditors' efforts, and the Standards carefully avoid imposing criteria on managers or board members. Standards for internal auditors can bind only internal auditors, and the Standards make it plain in the Introduction that implementation "will be governed by the environment in which the internal auditing department carries out its assigned responsibilities." But the Introduction states quite specifically that "compliance with the concepts enunciated by these Standards is essential before the responsibilities of internal auditors can be met."

The committee developing the Standards saw these purposes for their development—to establish a basis for consistent measurement of internal auditing operations; to unify internal auditing throughout the world; to encourage improved internal auditing; to assist in communicating to others the role, scope, performance, and objective of internal auditing; and to provide a vehicle by which internal auditing can be fully recognized as a profession. The Standards are divided into the following five sections:

1. Independence
2. Professional proficiency
3. Scope of work
4. Performance of audit work
5. Management of the internal audit department.

The following are some of the more significant concepts raised by the Standards (the numerical references identify the sections).

(i) 100. Independence
The Standards recognize the shift from "a service to management" to "a service to the organization." Organization in this sense comprises both management and the board of directors, and the Standards see the internal auditor as owing a duty to both.

The Standards point out the need for practical independence. Certainly, the internal auditor's paycheck is still signed by a member of management; but a concerted effort must be made to see that internal auditors in an organization are perceived to be independent of the activities they audit. To that end, the Standards point out that independence is enhanced when the board of directors concur in the appointment or removal of the director of internal auditing.

The Standards also recommend direct communication with the board of directors including the submission of reports showing the audit work was planned and accomplished, as well as the significant findings of the audit.

(ii) 200. Professional Proficiency

This section places requirements on both the internal auditing department and the internal auditor.

The Standards expect of the department reasonable assurance of the proficiency of prospective auditors, requiring the knowledge and skills within the department be sufficient to carry out audit responsibilities. The Standards require adequate supervision of the audit work.

Of the individual internal auditor the Standards expect compliance, skill in dealing with people and communicating audit results, the maintenance of technical competence through continuing education, and the exercise of professional care.

The Standards define "due professional care" in the same way as the courts would: "The care and skill expected of a reasonably prudent and competent internal auditor in the same or similar circumstances." This does not mean infallibility or extraordinary performance. It does not mean that the internal auditor can be held to be an insurer against all forms of wrongdoing within the enterprise. Such a responsibility for internal auditors would be as ludicrous as requiring a doctor to assure patients that they would never get sick or requiring a lawyer to assure clients that they would never be sued.

Due professional care requires alertness to the risk areas—to those potential conditions which promote or invite improprieties. To that extent, due professional care by internal auditors is not static. As the profession grows more sophisticated, as the literature expands to point out indicators or new ways of developing indicators of things amiss, the professional internal auditor will be expected to make use of them. If a new, specific drug for cancer were developed and hailed in the medical journals and approved by the Food and Drug Administration, and a doctor failed to prescribe it to a patient suffering from cancer where such a prescription was clearly indicated, the doctor could be held guilty of negligence.

Similarly, if internal auditors fail to make use of techniques their professional literature discusses and their peers are using to reveal wrongdoing, they could be considered negligent. The right to be called a professional carries burdens. One cannot claim the name without playing the game.

The drafters of the Standards were careful to point out that if internal auditors suspect irregularities, they should inform "the appropriate authorities within the organization." The Standards place no responsibility upon internal auditors to inform other authorities outside the organization.

(iii) 300. Scope of Work

Not all internal auditors have the charter or the skill to make a full-scope audit. The Standards recognize this, and the drafters were well aware that internal auditors must function within fences their superiors construct for them or else seek other forms or places of employment.

The Standards also state, at least implicitly, that the audit scope should ideally encompass four elements:

1. Integrity of information systems—accuracy, timeliness, and usefulness of accounting and operating records and reports.

2. Compliance with policies, plans, procedures, laws, and regulations—whether operating rules and regulations are still useful and appropriate.

3. Economical and efficient use of resources and safeguarding of assets—whether what is being done is done in the best way, and whether the resources of the organization are under adequate surveillance and control.

4. Adequacy of operating objectives and goals and the effectiveness of results—whether operating aims coincide with overall organizational aims, whether satisfactory objectives and goals are being met, whether assigned missions are being accomplished, and whether the control systems throughout the organization are functioning effectively and are designed to see that goals are being met.

The fourth element is the most difficult to accomplish because many auditors may not yet have the needed skills. Many organizations do not give their internal auditors that much authority, but professional internal auditing could not possibly turn its eyes away when an operation that is being done efficiently and economically is the wrong operation to begin with.

(iv) 400. Performance of Audit Work

The Standards expect certain qualities of performance from professional internal auditors. They should plan their work before they start it, and they should document those plans and their accomplishment. They should support their opinions and reports with sufficient, competent, and relevant information. The information should have enough depth to be compelling, have enough reliability to be believable, and have enough applicability to the issue at hand to be useful. The audit work accomplished should be reported to those entitled to know of it. And professional internal auditors are obligated to report findings and opinions clearly enough to be understood and compellingly enough to make the need for action evident.

Professional internal auditors should follow up their work to see that appropriate action is taken on reported audit findings. It is important to differentiate between "appropriate action . . .

on reported audit findings" on the one hand and "acceptance of internal audit recommendations" on the other. Managers are responsible for correcting defects in their organizations or operations in whatever manner they consider best; that is a management prerogative. Internal auditors are responsible for seeing that the defects have been corrected in whatever manner management considers appropriate.

(v) 500. Management of the Internal Auditing Department
Internal auditing departments have been managed as long as there have been internal auditing operations and managers. This section makes certain things about the auditing department specific and raises one new issue.

Made specific are establishing a charter for the department, planning for the audits to be carried out, providing policies and procedures to guide the staff, and staffing the department and training the people.

The new issue raised is the quality assurance program. Professional internal auditors are expected to provide for a review of their performance. They should be able to answer convincingly the question: "Who audits the internal auditors?" This is really not very different from the peer reviews made in academe. Peers are asked to review the work of academicians and express opinions on, whether academic standards are being met. Similar reviews are required for CPAs. The Standards propose three elements for a quality assurance program:

1. Current supervision of the audit work;

2. Internal reviews performed by one or more of the staff members who would examine the working papers and reports issued by other members of the staff;

3. External reviews by persons independent of the internal auditing department. Such reviews could be performed by internal auditors of other enterprises, by public accountants, or by qualified consultants. Many large internal auditing organizations have already undergone such reviews.

Questions are often raised about the difficulties faced by an internal auditing department made up of only one or two internal auditors. Obviously they would find it much more difficult to meet the Standards than would large internal auditing departments. Their scope of audit might be restricted by their charters. Direct supervision of the audit work could be difficult—or even impossible.

It is a problem, but if internal auditing is to be raised to the level of a learned profession, the standards must be high. Those internal auditors who are handicapped by lack of training or by the restrictive rules of their enterprises will have to strive harder to meet the standards if they aspire to professionalism.

(b) Statements on Internal Auditing Standards

Since the issuance of the original standards for the Professional Practice of Internal Auditing, the Professional Standards Committee of the Institute of Internal Auditors has periodically issued "Statements on Internal Auditing Standards" (SIAS). The Statements provide guidance and interpretations of the original standards.

The first Statement, No. 1, was published in July 1983 and since that date the Professional Standards Committee has periodically issued Statements including the following:

SIAS No. 1—Control: Concepts and Responsibilities

SIAS No. 2—Communicating Results

SIAS No. 3—Deterrence, Detection, Investigation, and Reporting of Fraud

SIAS No. 4—Quality Assurance

SIAS No. 5—Internal Auditors' Relationships with Independent Outside Auditors

SIAS No. 6—Audit Working Papers

SIAS No. 7—Communication with the Board of Directors

SIAS No. 8—Analytical Auditing Procedures

SIAS No. 9—Risk Assessment

SIAS No. 10—Evaluating Accomplishment of Established Objectives and Goals for Operations or Programs

SIAS No. 11—1992 Omnibus Statement

SIAS No. 12—Planning the Audit Assignment

SIAS No. 13—Follow-Up on Reported Audit Findings

The Statements are issued as exposure drafts for review. In 1989 the Institute of Internal Auditors issued the first codification of the Standards and Statements. This codification should be reviewed to see the current Standards.

(c) Summary of General and Specific Standards for the Practice of Internal Auditing

100 **Independence**—Internal auditors should be independent of the activities they audit.

110 *Organizational Status*—The organizational status of the internal auditing department should be sufficient to permit the accomplishment of its audit responsibilities.

120 *Objectivity*—Internal auditors should be objective in performing audits.

200 **Professional Proficiency**—Internal audits should be performed with proficiency and due professional care.

210 *The Internal Auditing Department Staffing*—The internal auditing department should provide assurance that the technical proficiency and educational background of internal auditors are appropriate for the audits to be performed.

220 *Knowledge, Skills, and Disciplines*—The internal auditing department should possess or should obtain the knowledge, skills, and disciplines needed to carry out its audit responsibilities.

230 *Supervision*—The internal auditing department should provide assurance that internal audits are properly supervised.

240 *The Internal Auditor Compliance with Standards of Conduct*—Internal auditors should comply with professional standards of conduct.

250 *Knowledge, Skills, and Disciplines*—Internal auditors should possess the knowledge, skills, and disciplines essential to the performance of internal audits.

260 *Human Relations and Communications*—Internal auditors should possess the knowledge, skills, and disciplines essential to the performance of internal audits.

270 *Continuing Education*—Internal auditors should maintain their technical competence through continuing education.

280 *Due Professional Care*—Internal auditors should exercise due professional care in performing internal audits.

300 **Scope of Work**—The scope of the internal audit should encompass the examination and evaluation of the adequacy and effectiveness of the organization's system of internal control, and the quality of performance in carrying out assigned responsibilities.

310 *Reliability and Integrity of Information*—Internal auditors should review the reliability and integrity of financial and operating information and the means used to identify, measure, classify, and report such information.

320 *Compliance with Policies, Plans, Procedures, Laws, and Regulations*—Internal auditors should review the systems established to ensure compliance with those policies, plans, procedures, laws, and regulations which could have a significant impact on operations and reports, and should determine whether the organization is in compliance.

330 *Safeguarding of Assets*—Internal auditors should review the means of safeguarding assets and, as appropriate, verify the existence of such assets.

340 *Economical and Efficient Use of Resources*—Internal auditors should appraise the economy and efficiency with which resources are employed.

350 *Accomplishment of Established Objectives and Goals for Operations or Programs*—Internal auditors should review operations or programs to ascertain whether results are consistent with established objectives and goals and whether the operations or programs are being carried out as planned.

400 **Performance of Audit Work**—Audit work should include planning the audit, examining and evaluating information, communicating results, and following up.

410 *Planning the Audit*—Internal auditors should plan each audit.

420 *Examining and Evaluating Information*—Internal auditors should collect, analyze, interpret, and document information to support audit results.

430 *Communicating Results*—Internal auditors should report the results of their audit work.

440 *Following Up*—Internal auditors should follow up to ascertain that appropriate action is taken on reported audit findings.

500 **Management of the Internal Auditing Department**—The Director of Internal Auditing should properly manage the internal auditing department.

510 *Purpose, Authority, and Responsibility*—The Director of Internal Auditing should have a statement of purpose, authority, and responsibility for the internal auditing department.

520 *Planning*—The Director of Internal Auditing should establish plans to carry out the responsibilities of the internal auditing department.

530 *Policies and Procedures*—The Director of Internal Auditing should provide written policies and procedures to guide the audit staff.

540 *Personnel Management and Development*—The Director of Internal Auditing should establish a program for selecting and developing the human resources of the internal auditing department.

550 *External Auditors*—The Director of Internal Auditing should coordinate internal and external audit efforts.

560 *Quality Assurance*—The Director of Internal Auditing should establish and maintain a quality assurance program to evaluate the operations of the internal auditing department.

(d)   Institute of Internal Auditors—Code of Ethics

Ethics involves dealing with what is good and what is bad and with moral duty and obligations. One of the hallmarks of a profession is having and following basic ethical standards. The Institute of Internal Auditors has published a Code of Ethics, see Figure 1.4, which is followed by IIA members and Certified Internal Auditors.

Figure 1.4   The Institute of Internal Auditors—Code of Ethics

PURPOSE: A distinguishing mark of a profession is acceptance by its members of responsibility to the interests of those it serves. Members of The Institute of Internal Auditors (Members) and Certified Internal Auditors (CIAs) must maintain high standards of conduct in order to effectively discharge this responsibility. The Institute of Internal Auditors (Institute) adopts this *Code of Ethics* for Members and CIAs.

APPLICABILITY: This *Code of Ethics* is applicable to all Members and CIAs. Membership in The Institute and acceptance of the "Certified Internal Auditor" designation are voluntary actions. By acceptance, Members and CIAs assume an obligation of self-discipline above and beyond the requirements of laws and regulations.

The standards of conduct set forth in this *Code of Ethics* provide basic principles in the practice of internal auditing. Members and CIAs should realize that their individual judgment is required in the application of these principles.

CIAs shall use the "Certified Internal Auditor" designation with discretion and in a dignified manner, fully aware of what the designation denotes. The designation shall also be used in a manner consistent with all statutory requirements.

Members who are judged by the Board of Directors of The Institute to be in violation of the standards of conduct of the *Code of Ethics* shall be subject to forfeiture of their membership in The Institute. CIAs who are similarly judged also shall be subject to forfeiture of the "Certified Internal Auditor" designation.

STANDARDS OF CONDUCT

I.   Members and CIAs shall exercise honesty, objectivity, and diligence in the performance of their duties and responsibilities.

II. Members and CIAs shall exhibit loyalty in all matters pertaining to the affairs of their organization or to whomever they may be rendering a service. However, Members and CIAs shall not knowingly be a party to any illegal or improper activity.

III. Members and CIAs shall not knowingly engage in acts or activities which are discreditable to the profession of internal auditing or to their organization.

IV. Members and CIAs shall refrain from entering into any activity which may be in conflict with the interest of their organization or which would prejudice their ability to carry out objectively their duties and responsibilities.

Figure 1.4 Continued

V.   Members and CIAs shall not accept anything of value from an employee, client, customer, supplier, or business associate of their organization which would impair or be presumed to impair their professional judgment.

VI.   Members and CIAs shall undertake only those services which they can reasonably expect to complete with professional competence.

VII.   Members and CIAs shall adopt suitable means to comply with the *Standards for the Professional Practice of Internal Auditing.*

VIII.   Members and CIAs shall be prudent in the use of information acquired in the course of their duties. They shall not use confidential information for any personal gain nor in any manner which would be contrary to law or detrimental to the welfare of their organization.

IX.   Members and CIAs, when reporting on the results of their work, shall reveal all material facts known to them which, if not revealed, could either distort reports of operations under review or conceal unlawful practices.

X.   Members and CIAs shall continually strive for improvement in their proficiency, and in the effectiveness and quality of their service.

XI.   Members and CIAs, in the practice of their profession, shall be ever mindful of their obligation to maintain the high standards of competence, morality, and dignity promulgated by The Institute. Members shall abide by the *Bylaws* and uphold the objectives of The Institute.

Adapted by the IIA Board of Directors, July 1988.

1.6 RESPONSIBILITIES OF A CORPORATE AUDITOR

(a) Nature

Internal auditing is an independent appraisal activity within an organization for the review of operations as a service to management. It improves managerial control by measuring and evaluating the effectiveness of other controls.

(b) Objective and Scope

The objective of internal auditing is to assist all members of the organization in the effective discharge of responsibilities by furnishing them with analyses, appraisals, recommendations, and pertinent comments concerning the activities reviewed. The internal auditor is concerned with any phase of business activity where he/she may provide service to the organization. This involves going beyond the accounting and financial records to obtain a full understanding of the operations under review. The attainment of this overall objective involves such activities as:

- Reviewing and appraising the soundness, adequacy, and application of accounting, financial, and other operating controls and promoting effective control at reasonable cost

- Ascertaining the extent of compliance with established policies, plans, and procedures

- Ascertaining the extent to which company assets are accounted for and safeguarded from losses of all kinds

- Ascertaining the reliability of management data developed within the organization

- Ascertaining the quality of performance in carrying out assigned responsibilities

- Recommending operational improvements.

(c) Responsibility and Authority

The responsibilities of corporate auditing within Sam Pole Company are clearly established by management policy. The related authority provides the corporate auditor full access to all of the organization's records, properties, and personnel relevant to the subject under review. The corporate auditor should be free to review and appraise policies, plans, procedures, and records.

The internal auditor's responsibilities should be:

- To inform and advise management and to discharge this responsibility in a manner that is consistent with the Code of Ethics of the IIA

- To coordinate his/her activities with others so as to best achieve audit objectives and the objectives of the organization.

A corporate auditor has neither direct responsibility for nor authority over any of the activities which he reviews. Therefore, the corporate audit review and appraisal do not in any way relieve other persons in the organization of the responsibilities assigned to them.

(d) Independence

Independence is essential to the effectiveness of corporate auditing. This independence is obtained primarily through organizational status and objectivity:

> The organizational status of the corporate auditing function and the support accorded to it by management are major determinants of its range and value. The head of the corporate auditing function should be responsible to an officer whose authority is sufficient to assure both a broad range of audit coverage and the adequate consideration of and effective action on the audit findings and recommendations.

Objectivity is essential to the audit function. Therefore, a corporate auditor should not develop and install procedures, prepare records, or engage in any other activity which he would normally review and could reasonably be construed to compromise his independence. His or her objectivity need not be adversely affected by his determination and recommendation of standards to be applied in the development of the systems and procedures under review.

It is common to read in the financial section of a newspaper or other publication that a public accounting firm was being sued or censored. Why? Because it was alleged that the audit did not follow generally accepted standards or that the report on financial statements was not accurate or did not disclose certain information required by the Securities and Exchange Commission (SEC) or other regulatory body that could influence shareholders and/or the general public in financial planning decisions.

Although similar situations specifically addressed to the internal audit profession are rare, the possibility does exist. The SEC and other regulatory organizations are looking in that direction due to the improved image of the profession and the greater reliance upon internal auditors' work by management and the public accountants.

Don't be alarmed! Unlike the public accountants, internal auditors do not have the same contractual or fiduciary obligations. We do have similar responsibilities. Therefore, we must perform our audits with the same extreme care as they do, and in accordance with generally accepted auditing standards.

The Director of Auditing reports directly to the Audit Committee of the Board of Directors of Sam Pole Company for the purposes of audit scope. The Director's responsibility to the Committee, the entire Board of Directors, and management is to inform them promptly of significant situations disclosed by audit so that they can meet their obligations to the shareholders, regulatory bodies, and the general public. Also, the "Foreign Corrupt Practices Act," which was passed in 1977, requires, under penalty of law, that managements ensure good systems of internal control in their companies.

(e) Regulatory Issues

Due care is required in reporting comments related to regulatory bodies. For example, the Internal Revenue Service can and does request copies of audit reports during their examinations of tax returns. The company's reporting should be objective and factual to reduce further extensive tests of expense reports. If improved controls for reporting of travel and other business expenses are recommended, it is essential that the situations are clearly described and the number of instances noted be reflected in the detailed section of the audit report. Also the corrective action taken, if any, should be indicated. Otherwise, the auditee will normally do so in the response to the audit report.

The company's legal responsibilities can be attained if due care is used, generally accepted auditing standards are followed, situations are promptly and carefully reported, and confidentiality is maintained.

(i) Introduction

Recognizing that ethics are an important consideration in the practice of internal auditing and that the moral principles followed by members of the Institute of Internal Auditors should be formalized, the Board of Directors at its regular meeting in New Orleans on December 13, 1968, received and adopted the following resolution:

Whereas The members of the Institute of Internal Auditors, represent the profession of internal auditing; and

Whereas managements rely on the profession of internal auditing to assist in the fulfillment of their management stewardship; and

Whereas said members must maintain high standards of conduct, honor, and character in order to carry on proper and meaningful internal auditing practice;

Therefore Be It Resolved that a Code of Ethics be now set forth, outlining the standards of professional behavior for the guidance of each member of the Institute of Internal Auditors, Inc.

In accordance with this resolution, the Board of Directors further approved of the principles set forth.

(ii) Interpretation of Principles

The provisions of the Code of Ethics cover basic principles in the various disciplines of internal auditing practice. Members shall realize that individual judgment is required in the application of these principles. They have a responsibility to conduct themselves so that their good faith and integrity should not be open to question. While having due regard to the limit of their technical skills, they will promote the highest possible internal auditing standards to the end of advancing the interest of their company or organization.

(iii) Articles

I. Members shall have an obligation to exercise honesty, objectivity, and diligence in the performance of their duties and responsibilities.

II. Members, in holding the trust of their employers, shall exhibit loyalty in all matters pertaining to the affairs of the employer or to whomever they may be rendering a service. However, members shall not knowingly be a part to any illegal or improper activity.

III. Members shall refrain from entering into any activity that may be in conflict with the interest of their employers or would prejudice their ability to carry out objectively their duties and responsibilities.

IV. Members shall not accept a fee or a gift from an employee, a client, a customer or a business and associate of their employer without the knowledge and consent of their senior management.

V. Members shall be prudent in the use of information acquired in the course of their duties. They shall not use confidential information for any personal gain nor in a manner that would be detrimental to the welfare of their employer.

VI. Members, in expressing an opinion, shall use all reasonable care to obtain sufficient factual evidence to warrant such expression. In their reporting, members shall reveal such material facts known to them which, if not revealed, could either distort the report of the results of operations under review or conceal unlawful practice.

VII. Members shall continually strive for improvement in the proficiency and effectiveness of their service.

VIII. Members shall abide by the bylaws and uphold the objectives of The Institute of Internal Auditors. In the practice of their profession, they shall be ever mindful of their obligation to maintain the high standard of competence, morality and dignity which The Institute of Internal Auditors and its members have established.

1.7 STANDARDS FOR INFORMATION SYSTEMS AUDITING

(a) Adoption of Standards

(i) The Information Systems Audit & Control Association—ISACA (Formerly the EDP Auditors Association) and the Information Systems Audit and Control Foundation—ISACF (Formerly the EDP Auditors Foundation)

The concept of a professional association of computer auditors originated in Los Angeles, California, in the late 1960s with a small group of auditors who were working in the area of computerized systems. They believed that, with computer-based systems becoming an integral part of the managerial and financial operations of their organizations, and with such systems growing in size and complexity, there was a great need to develop auditing capability in this area. They envisioned filling this need by sharing experiences and ideas with fellow practitioners, and by developing training courses and educational materials to assist others who were assigned similar audit responsibilities.

That their idea was one whose time had come is witnessed by the fact that the organization they founded, The EDP Auditors Association, Inc., now the ISACA has become a worldwide organization of Information Systems Audit professionals, representing both internal and external auditing, working in all areas of private industry and government.

Since its founding in 1969, the ISACA has been dedicated to the promotion of research, education and certification for information systems auditing. Its prime objectives are to provide a forum for its members, which encourages a free exchange of information systems auditing knowledge and skills, and to assist individuals in their professional development and growth.

The EDP Auditors Foundation (EDPAF), founded in 1976, now the ISACF was established to engage in educational activities and research in the field of information systems auditing.

The objectives of the Foundation are to:

- Develop and maintain professional standards for information systems auditing

- Conduct research in information systems auditing and computer controls

- Assist professionals in the study of auditing and information systems.

At its 1985 Annual Membership Meeting held during the Association's International Conference in Salt Lake City, Utah, the general membership of the EDPAA approved the establishment of a Standards Board and charged that board with the responsibility to set standards for the professional practice of information systems auditing.

(ii) General

Computer based systems are useful and pervasive tools applied in the management and operation of many organizations. Such systems may effect control over many of the assets and operations of an organization. Development and support of such systems may require a significant portion of an organization's total resources. When these conditions exist, the auditor's mission may include auditing the development, maintenance and operation of the systems.

The work of auditors, both external and internal, is governed in general by standards developed by a number of professional organizations, each of which seeks to assure the quality of auditing work being performed.

(iii)   Need for Information Systems Auditing Standards
The standards of these professional organizations apply to the work of their members, in relation to the nature of the audit work involved. The ISACF has determined that the specialized nature of information systems auditing work, and the skills necessary to perform such audits, require the development and promulgation of auditing standards which apply specifically to information systems auditing.

(iv)   Definition of Information Systems Auditing
For purposes of these standards, information systems auditing is defined as any audit that encompasses the review and evaluation of all aspects (or any portion) of automated information processing systems, including related non-automated processes, and the interfaces between them.

Information systems auditors review and evaluate the development, maintenance and operation of components of automated systems (or such systems as a whole) and their interfaces with the non-automated areas of the organization's operations. The objectives of such auditing generally are to assess the extent to which such systems or components produce reliable and accurate information and to determine if such information is in conformity with management's requirements and any applicable statutory provisions.

(v)   The Standards Board and Its Operations
The Standards Board is a standing committee of the ISACF, and is composed of both elected and appointed positions. Of its nine members, five are Foundation trustees who hold their board position ex officio, and four are "outside" members. The EDPAA Vice President for Standards (a trustee of the Foundation and Chairperson of the Standards Board), proposes outside members of appointment to the Board; such proposed appointments are effective upon confirmation by the Foundation's Board of Trustees. The term of an outside member is generally three years, subject to annual renewal by the Board of Trustees.

The Board's formally adopted mission is as follows:

> *To advance the quality of information systems auditing, it is the responsibility of the Standards Board to promulgate and maintain standards of practice. These standards apply to members of the EDP Auditors Association and to holders of the Certificate in Information Systems Auditing.*

The Board thus defines, develops and promulgates standards, interpretations of standards, guide-lines, procedures and other information relating to standards for the professional practice of Information Systems Auditing. It performs this work through a Standards Committee (composed of appointed members of the EDP Auditors Association), through task forces, and through control review groups which make up a representative cross section of the information systems audit profession.

(vi) Board Procedures

Prior to promulgation of a standard, an Exposure Draft document is distributed in several phases to a broad base of information systems audit professionals to solicit comments. The purpose of releasing an Exposure Draft to practitioners is to test the standard and determine that it achieves its intended purpose. It is the responsibility of the Board, working through the Standards Committee, to ensure that all comments are reviewed and considered. The ultimate decision regarding format, content, scope and effective date of a standard rests with the Board. Promulgation of a standard requires a two-thirds majority affirmative vote of the Board.

(vii) Authority Attached to the Standards

The standards' authority is derived from the Code of Professional Ethics (Figure 1.5), which pro-vides that members of the EDP Auditors Association and holders of the Certificate in Information Systems Auditing will comply with information systems auditing standards adopted by the EDP Auditors Foundation. Non-compliance with these standards could result in termination of an individual's membership in the EDP Auditors Association and, in the case of a Certified Informa-tion Systems Auditor, revocation of the individual's certification.

The authority of guidelines and procedures is secondary to the standards themselves, and the extent of such authority will be detailed in each issuance.

(viii) Relationship between Information Systems Auditing Standards and Other Auditing Standards

Information systems auditing standards promulgated by the ISACF are not intended to supersede the auditing standards or regulations developed by other professional organizations or by govern-mental bodies. In any situation where a conflict is perceived to exist between the standards of the ISACF and those of another body, it is the auditor's responsibility to use professional judgment, based upon the specific facts in the situation, to resolve the matter.

(ix) Language

The official text of standards and other standards related information promulgated by the ISACF is that text approved by the Board in the English language. Chapters and Regions of the EDP Auditors Association are authorized to prepare translations of this material in their own language, as deemed appropriate by them, but such translations should indicate the name of the group making them. The translated document should contain an explicit statement that it is a translation of the approved English text.

(b)   General Standards for Information Systems Auditing

(i)   Introduction

The ISACF has determined that the specialized nature of information systems auditing and the skills necessary to perform such audits require the development and promulgation of Information Systems Auditing Standards which apply specifically to information systems auditing.

Information systems auditing is defined as any audit that encompasses the review and evaluation of all aspects (or any portion) of automated information processing systems, including related non-automated processes, and the interfaces between them.

Standards promulgated by the ISACF are applicable to information systems auditing work performed by members of the ISACA, and by holders of the Certificate in Information Systems Auditing.

Further background concerning the EDP Auditors Association, the EDP Auditors Foundation, and their information systems auditing standards program is contained in the "Preface to General Standards for Information Systems Auditing and Statements on Information Systems Auditing Standards."

(ii)   Objectives

The objectives of these standards are to inform auditors of the minimum level of acceptable performance required to meet the professional responsibilities set forth in the Code of Professional Ethics and to inform management and other interested parties of the profession's expectations concerning the work of practitioners.

(iii)   General Standards for Information Systems Auditing

The following ten standards are applicable to information systems auditing as defined above.

Independence

General Standard No. 1: **Attitude and Appearance**—In all matters related to auditing, the information systems auditor is to be independent of the auditee in attitude and appearance.

General Standard No. 2: **Organizational Relationship**—The information systems audit function is to be sufficiently independent of the area being audited to permit objective completion of the audit.

General Standard No. 3: **Code of Professional Ethics**—The information systems auditor is to adhere to the Code of Professional Ethics of the EDP Auditors Foundation.

Technical Competence

General Standard No. 4: **Skills and Knowledge**—The information systems auditor is to be technically competent, possessing the skills and knowledge necessary in the performance of the auditor's work.

General Standard No. 5: **Continuing Professional Education**—The information systems auditor is to maintain technical competence through appropriate continuing education.

Performance of Work

General Standard No. 6: **Planning and Supervision**—Information systems audits are to be planned and supervised to provide assurance that audit objectives are achieved and compliance with these standards is met.

General Standard No. 7: **Evidence Requirement**—During the course of the audit, the information systems auditor is to obtain evidence of a nature and sufficiency to support findings and conclusions reported.

General Standard No. 8: **Due Professional Care**—Due professional care is to be exercised in all aspects of the information systems auditor's work, including observance of applicable auditing standards.

Reporting

General Standard No. 9: **Reporting of Audit Coverage**—In preparing reports, the information systems auditor is to state the objectives of the audit, the period of coverage and the nature and extent of the audit work performed.

General Standard No. 10: **Reporting of Findings and Conclusions**—In preparing reports, the information systems auditor is to state findings and conclusions concerning the audit work performed and any reservations or qualifications that the auditor has with respect to the audit.

(iv) Effective Date

These standards are effective for all information systems audits with period of coverage beginning January 1, 1988.

(c) Statements on Information Systems Auditing Standards

Since the issuance of the original standards for the professional practice of EDP auditing, the standards board of the ISACF has periodically issued Statements on Information Systems Auditing Standards. The statements provide guidance and interpretation of the original standards.

The first statement, (1) was published in April, 1989, and since that date, the standards board has periodically issued statements including the following:

SISAS #1—Independence—Attitude and Appearance Organization Relationship

SISAS #2—Independence—Involvement in the Systems Development Process

SAM POLE COMPANY

CORPORATE AUDIT DEPARTMENT		
PROCEDURES MANUAL	DATE:	
TITLE: Standards for Information Systems Auditing	NO: 1.7	PAGES:

SISAS #3—Performance of Work—Evidence Requirement

SISAS #4—Performance of Work—Due Professional Care

SISAS #5—Performance of Work—The Use of Risk Assessment in Audit Planning

SISAS #6—Performance of Work—Audit Documentation

SISAS #7—Reporting—Audit Reports

SISAS #8—Performance of Work—Audit Consideration for Irregularities

SISAS #9—Performance of Work—Use of Audit Software Tools

(d) Information Systems Audit and Control Foundation: Code of Professional Ethics

Ethics involves dealing with moral duty and obligations. One of the hallmarks of a profession is having and following basic ethical standards. The Information Systems Audit & Control Foundation has published a Code of Professional Ethics, see Figure 1.5, which is followed by Information Systems Audit & Control Association members and Certified Information Systems Auditors.

Figure 1.5   Information Systems Audit and Control Foundation—Code of Professional Ethics

The ISAC Foundation, Inc., sets forth this Code of Professional Ethics to guide the professional and personal conduct of members of the ISAC Association and/or holders of the Certificate in Information Systems Auditing.

Information systems auditors shall:

1. Support the establishment of and compliance with appropriate standards, procedures, and controls for information systems.

2. Comply with Information Systems Auditing Standards as adopted by the ISAC Foundation.

3. Serve in the interest of their employers, stockholders, clients and the general public in a diligent, loyal and honest manner, and shall not knowingly be a party to any illegal or improper activities.

4. Maintain the confidentiality of information obtained in the course of their duties. This information shall not be used for personal benefit nor released to inappropriate parties.

5. Perform their duties in an independent and objective manner, and shall avoid activities which threaten, or may appear to threaten, their independence.

6. Maintain competency in the interrelated fields of auditing and information systems through participation in professional development activities.

7. Use due care to obtain and document sufficient factual material on which to base conclusions and recommendations.

8. Inform the appropriate parties of the results of audit work performed.

9. Support the education of management, clients, and the general public to enhance their understanding of auditing and information systems.

10. Maintain high standards of conduct and character in both professional and personal activities.

Reprinted with permission of ISACF.

Chapter 2

AUDIT PLANNING

2.1 CORPORATE AUDIT PLANNING, SCHEDULING, AND STAFFING
    (a) Three-Year Operating Plan
        (i) Auditable Units
    (b) Risk Analysis
    (c) Annual Budget and Plan
        (i) Annual Department Budget
        (ii) Annual Audit Plan
    (d) Six-Month Audit Plan
    (e) Three-Month Audit Schedule
    (f) Two-Month Staff Schedule

2.2 EVALUATING INTERNAL CONTROLS
    (a) Definitions and Basic Concepts
        (i) Study of Internal Control System
        (ii) Evaluation of System
        (iii) Correlation with Other Auditing Procedures

2.3 MATERIALITY

2.4 TYPES OF AUDITS
    (a) High-Level Review of Procedures
    (b) Financial Audit
    (c) Operational/Managerial Audit
    (d) Compliance Audit
    (e) Contract Audit
    (f) Desk Review
    (g) Follow-Up Audits
    (h) EDP Audits
    (i) International Audits

2.5 TIME REPORTING
    (a) Form: Corporate Audit Time Report
    (b) Report for the Period Ending
    (c) Auditor's Name/Employee Number
    (d) Job Number

      (e)   Audit Codes
      (f)   Task Codes
      (g)   Hours
      (h)   Productive Time
      (i)   Nonproductive Time
      (j)   Summarizing Time

2.6   EXPENSE REPORTING
      (a)   Travel Expenses

2.1 CORPORATE AUDIT PLANNING, SCHEDULING, AND STAFFING

Planning is a very basic element of all business activities. The Audit Department is no exception. The long-term departmental operating plan will demonstrate an organized approach to systematically auditing all company operations. In our example, we have developed a three-year operating plan. We would discuss the extended cycle of audit coverage with management and, if appropriate, with the Audit Committee. This would establish our overall game plan for auditing company locations. In many companies, every aspect of the company's operations should be audited, to some extent (see Types of Audits, Section 2.4), on a formal rotation basis. Even small operations should be considered for audit visits. The audit "deterrent factor" should not be underestimated.

The planning matrix (Figure 2.1) illustrates the flow and relationship of the three-year plan to the annual operating budget, six-month audit plan, three-month audit schedule and two-month staff schedule. By beginning with the long-term planning exercise, the work investment naturally flows down to the planning for the shorter periods. Here is where we look for integration of our activities to save work down the line. In formulating the three-year plan, we should consider the subsequent shorter term plans by developing a long term in six-month or other appropriate sub-periods to feed into the shorter term planning process.

(a) Three-Year Operating Plan

One of the responsibilities designated by the Corporate Audit Charter is for the Director of Auditing of the corporation to establish a plan of audit. The three-year audit plan (Figure 2.2) provides long-term forecasting. It also establishes the coverage of audits for a three-year cycle approach to total coverage of companies within the company.

The three-year plan optimizes staffing requirements and the cost effectiveness of the Audit Department. The plan is based upon materiality and exposure to risk for establishing priorities of the audit entities and number of hours for the audits.

The three-year plan may be developed in detailed increments of six-month time periods. Circumstances that affect change to the plan are management request and detailed monthly planning.

(i) Auditable Units
In order to develop an audit plan, a company's auditable unit must be selected. An audit unit can be a subsidiary operation, a department, a division, a system, or even an account. For instance, the XYZ Company may be audited. Alternatively, the XYZ Company's sales/accounts receivable/cash receipts system can be audited or its accounts receivable balance can be subject to audit verification. A logical approach for each company must be developed. In many cases, combinations of audit types will result. Often, various audit units at a specific location will be combined to create a logical audit unit.

Figure 2.1   Corporate Audit Planning, Scheduling, and Staffing

	THREE-YEAR OPERATING PLAN	ANNUAL BUDGET AND PLAN	SIX-MONTH AUDIT PLAN	THREE-MONTH AUDIT SCHEDULE	TWO-MONTH STAFF SCHEDULE
PURPOSE	Document department operating plan for Audit Committee and Management. Coordinate audit coverage with public accountants.	Forecast calendar year audit plan as basis for financial budget	Plan detail of audit assignments: nature of audit; scope; timing; manpower	Schedule three-month segment of six-month plan	Notify supervision and staff of assignment schedules
BASIS	Owner's request to provide total coverage of principal audit areas over a three-year cycle. Audit management decision regarding rotation.	Audit plans: Second half current year; first half next year. Manpower, traveling, professional development and administration costs. Audit management discretion	Specific implementation of each six-month period of the three-year plan. Budget constraints. Audit management discretion	Attainable audit objectives for three months based upon six-month plan. Management discretion.	Three-month audit schedule. Manager discretion.
TIMING REVISION	Timing: Annually in August	Timing: Annually in August	Timing: Semiannually: 60 days prior to six-month period	Timing: Beginning of first month for each three-month period Revision: As required	Timing: Beginning of first month of each two-month period, Administrative Assistant to staff Revision: As required
RESPONSIBILITY	Primary – Manager – P&C Secondary – Sr.	Primary – Manager – P&C Secondary – Sr.	Primary – Manager – P&C Secondary – Sr.	Primary – Manager – P&C Secondary – Sr.	Primary – Manager Secondary – Sr.

Figure 2.2 Sample Three-Year Audit Plan

Sam Pole Company
Corporate Audit Department
Three-year Audit Plan

National Brand
45-664 EyeEase 2 - Pack
45-384
Made in USA

| Audit Unit Number | Audit Unit | Risk Factor X Wgt. 1 | Risk Factor X Wgt. 2 | Risk Factor X Wgt. 3 | Risk Profile | Estimated Audit Hours Jan.–June 199X | July–Dec. 199X | Jan.–June 199X+1 | July–Dec. 199X+1 | Jan.–June 199X+2 | July–Dec. 199X+2 |

(b) Risk Analysis

The objective to cover all company operations over a period or cycle can be difficult to achieve. Of course, the number of personnel required on the staff to achieve this objective will need to be calculated. In order to develop the plan further, some type of risk analysis will be required. Some of the factors to consider in a risk analysis include: size of the operations (assets or revenues), results of prior audits, types of inventories, and many other considerations. Some internal audit departments develop sophisticated models to analyze potential risk and integrate that into their long-range plan. Some form of risk analysis should be utilized in every planning document.

Depending on your company's specific operations and management concerns, the various risk factors are identified in the plan. Care must be taken to analyze the cost versus benefit of a complex risk base audit plan. Many risk analyses result in a potentially complex summary of mostly subjective criteria, such as results of previous audits or the control concern level of management, and a restatement of obvious objective criteria, such as materiality. However a basic summary of risk analysis should be performed. Since all risks are not equal, each risk factor is assigned a weighting factor. The following is an example:

Risk Factor	Weight Factor (5=highest–1=lowest)
Materiality	5
Results of Prior Audits	3

For each audit unit, a score for each risk factor should be developed and multiplied by the risk factor weighting. For instance, a scale of 5 to 1 can be used with 5 representing high risk and 1 representing low risk or a good control environment. The following is an example:

Risk Factor	Weight Factor (5=highest–1=lowest)	Risk Score
Materiality	5	5
Results of Previous Audits	3	1

From this type of analysis, a risk profile can be developed to support decisions of audit frequency or scope. Finally, audit review and management judgment should be applied to the plan and risk assessment. All audit managers should be encouraged to provide input and review.

(c) Annual Budget and Plan

The company utilizes many budgets to operate its various companies, divisions, and so forth. Local budgets consolidate into corporate budgets, production forecasts, capital appropriation budgets, and many others. Auditing, along with all other departments, within the company must comply with these accounting practices.

SAM POLE COMPANY	(LOGO)	CORPORATE AUDIT DEPARTMENT	
		PROCEDURES MANUAL	DATE:

TITLE: Planning, Scheduling, and Staffing   NO: 2.1   PAGES:

Departmental budgets and plans are the direct responsibility of the Director of Auditing. Departmental budgets and plans include the annual departmental budget, the three-year audit plan, annual audit plan, and monthly staff assignments. Each kind of plan is discussed in more detail in subsequent sections.

(i)   Annual Department Budget

The annual departmental budget is requested by the Audit Committee each fiscal year. The Director of Auditing must present the departmental budget as a Corporate Cost Center to the chief financial officer and the corporate budget department after the Audit Committee has approved it.

The annual departmental budget covers all facets of the department's expenditures for the following calendar year. This includes number of personnel, salaries, salary raises, supplies, conferences, travel, employment fees, benefits, and several other expenses. Once the budget is developed and approved, it becomes difficult to substantially change the direction of the department such that additional costs will be incurred.

(ii)   Annual Audit Plan

An annual audit plan is primarily developed from the three-year plan and becomes a determinant in preparing the department budget. The annual audit plan is principally a summary of the next two applicable six-month periods of the three-year plan. The annual plan is used to support the manpower and travel expense estimates used in the annual budget.

(d)   Six-Month Audit Plan

Most audit departments prepare an annual audit plan. Our example is broken down into six-month modules to provide for synchronization with external auditors (if applicable). Most external auditors plan for the next annual audit in the spring (assuming a calendar year end). This may inhibit coordination if the internal audit plan is fixed for the calendar year. Therefore, the internal audit plan is projected for the year, but fixed in six-month modules to provide for some flexibility in the second half of the year.

This flexibility is also desirable in order to be able to plan audits consistent with changes in the company's direction.

(e)   Three-Month Audit Schedule

The six-month plan is used to develop the department schedule for the next three months. The schedules are required to be in place at the beginning of each three-month period. Nevertheless, it is desirable that they be prepared at least fifteen days before the beginning of the period.

(f)   Two-Month Staff Schedule

For the purpose of providing as much advance notice of pending audits as possible, a "Corporate Audit Staff Schedule" form is completed two months in advance for distribution.

The form is designed by listing staff along the left side of the form and days of the month across the top. Assignments are written for each staff member across this matrix. The schedule allows the staff to plan the beginning of audits and project travel assignments for personnel purposes.

Although the best intentions and forethought go into developing the Corporate Audit staff schedule, not all circumstances can be anticipated. The auditee may require or request a different time period for their audit than that scheduled. Management may request an audit not previously scheduled or change the timing of others. It means that auditors must remain flexible.

When scheduling changes affect your plans, it may be possible to make other arrangements. Contact the Internal Audit Manager to see what can be worked out.

SAM POLE COMPANY	(LOGO)	CORPORATE AUDIT DEPARTMENT	
		PROCEDURES MANUAL	DATE:

TITLE: Evaluating Internal Controls	NO: 2.2	PAGES:

2.2 EVALUATING INTERNAL CONTROLS

(a) Definitions and Basic Concepts

Section 310 of Standards for the Professional Practice of Internal Auditing addresses the reliability and integrity of information. The section states, "Internal auditors should review the reliability and integrity of financial and operating information and the means used to identify, measure, classify, and report such information." Encompassed in this definition are internal controls.

Internal controls in the broad sense include controls that may be characterized as either administrative or accounting, as follows:

A. *Administrative Control*—This includes, but is not limited to the plan of organization and the procedures and records that are concerned with the decision-making processes leading to management's authorization of transactions.

B. *Accounting Control*—This comprises the plan of organization and the procedures and records that are concerned with the safeguarding of assets and the reliability of financial records. They are designed to provide reasonable assurance that:

    a. Transactions are authorized

    b. Transactions are recorded

        1. In accordance with generally accepted accounting principles and other statements

        2. Accountability for assets is maintained

    c. Access to assets is controlled

    d. The recorded accountability for assets is compared with existing assets at reasonable intervals.

C. *Management Responsibility*—It is management's responsibility to establish and maintain a system of internal control. The system of internal control should be under continuing supervision by management to determine that it is functioning as prescribed and is modified as appropriate for changes in conditions.

D. *Reasonable Assurance*—The concept recognizes that the cost of internal control should not exceed the benefits expected to be derived. The benefits consist of reductions in the risk of failing to achieve the objectives implicit in the definition of accounting control.

E. *Methods of Data Processing*—Since the definition and related basic concepts of accounting control are expressed in terms of objectives, they are independent of the method of processing used; consequently, they apply equally to manual, mechanical, and electronic data processing systems.

F. *Limitations*—There are inherent limitations that should be recognized in considering the potential effectiveness of any system of accounting control. In the performance of most control procedures, there are possibilities for errors arising from causes such as misunderstanding instructions and mistakes of judgment, personal carelessness, distraction, or fatigue. Furthermore, procedures whose effectiveness depends on the segregation of duties obviously can be circumvented by collusion. Similarly, procedures designed to assure the execution and recording of transactions in accordance with management's authorizations may be ineffective against either errors or irregularities perpetrated by management with respect to transactions or to the estimates and judgements required in the preparation of financial statements. In addition to the limitations discussed above, any projection of a current evaluation of internal accounting control to future periods is subject to the risk that the procedures may become inadequate because of changes in conditions and that the degree of compliance with the procedures may deteriorate.

G. *Personnel*—Reasonable assurance that the objectives of accounting control are achieved depends on the competence and integrity of personnel, the independence of their assigned functions, and their understanding of the prescribed procedures. Although these factors are important, their contribution is to provide an environment conducive to accounting control rather than to provide assurance that it necessarily will be achieved.

H. *Segregation of Functions*—Incompatible functions for accounting control purposes are those that place any person in a position both to perpetrate and to conceal errors or irregularities in the normal course of his duties. Anyone who records transactions or has access to assets ordinarily is in a position to perpetrate errors or irregularities. For example, anyone who records disbursements could omit the recording of a check, either unintentionally or intentionally. If the same person also reconciles the bank account, the failure to record a check could be concealed through an improper reconciliation.

I. *Execution of Transactions*—Obtaining reasonable assurance that transactions are executed as authorized requires independent evidence that authorizations are issued by persons acting within the scope of their authority and that transactions conform with the terms of the authorizations. These terms may be either explicit or implicit, the latter being in the form of company policies or usual business practices applicable to the transactions involved. In some cases the required evidence is obtained by independent comparison of transaction documents with specific authorizations. For example, receiving reports and vendors' invoices may be compared with purchase orders in approving vouchers for payments; further, paid checks may be compared with approved vouchers, either individually or collectively, through reconciliations and related procedures. In other cases, such comparisons may be made with general authorizations such as general price lists, credit policies, or automatic reorder points. Such comparisons may be made manually or by computers. Reasonable assurance may sometimes be obtained by comparison of recorded transactions with budgets or standard costs, but the effectiveness of this alternative depends on the extent to which variations are identified and investigated. In some cases the only practicable means for obtaining reasonable assurance is by periodic surveillance of the personnel engaged in the execution of transactions.

J. *Recording of Transactions*—The objective of accounting control with respect to the recording of transactions requires that they be recorded at the amounts and in the accounting periods in which they were executed and be classified in appropriate accounts. For this purpose accounting periods refer to the periods for which financial statements are to be prepared. In the definition of accounting control this objective is expressed in terms of permitting, rather than assuring, the preparation of financial statements in conformity with generally accepted accounting principles (GAAP) or any other applicable criteria. This distinction recognizes that, beyond the necessary recording of transactions, management judgment is required in making estimates and other decisions required in the preparation of such statements.

K. *Access to Assets*—The objective of safeguarding assets requires that access to assets be limited to authorized personnel. In this context, access to assets includes both direct physical access and indirect access through the preparation or processing of documents that authorize the use or disposition of assets. Access to assets is required, of course, in the normal operations of a business and, therefore, limiting access to authorized personnel is the maximum constraint that is feasible for accounting control purposes in this respect. The number and caliber of personnel to whom access is authorized should be influenced by the nature of the assets and the related susceptibility to loss through errors and irregularities. Limitation of direct access to assets requires appropriate physical segregation and protective equipment or devices.

L. *Comparison of Recorded Accountability with Assets*—The purpose of comparing recorded accountability with assets is to determine whether the actual assets agree with the recorded accountability, and consequently, it is closely related to the foregoing discussion concerning the recording of transactions. Typical examples of this comparison include cash and securities counts, bank reconciliations, and physical inventories.*

---

*Standards for the Professional Practice of Internal Auditing by The Institute of Internal Auditors, copyright 1978 by The Institute of Internal Auditors, Inc., 290 Maitland Avenue, Altamonte Springs, Florida 32701, U.S.A. Reprinted with permission.

If comparison reveals that assets do not agree with the recorded accountability, it provides evidence of unrecorded or improperly recorded transactions. The converse, however, does not necessarily follow. For example, agreement of a cash count with the recorded balance does not provide evidence that all cash received has been properly recorded. This illustrates an unavoidable distinction between fiduciary and recorded accountability. The former arises immediately upon acquisition of an asset; the latter arises only when the initial record of the transaction is prepared.

As to assets that are susceptible to loss through errors or irregularities, the comparison with recorded accountability should be made independently. The frequency with which such comparison should be made for the purpose of safeguarding assets depends on the nature and amount of the assets involved and the cost of making a comparison.

The frequency with which the comparison of recorded accountability with assets should be made for the purpose of achieving reliability of the records for preparing financial statements depends on the materiality of the assets and their susceptibility to loss through errors or irregularities.

The action that may be appropriate with respect to any discrepancies revealed by the comparison of recorded accountability with assets will depend primarily on the nature of the asset, the system in use, and the amount and cause of the discrepancy. Appropriate action may include adjustment of the accounting records, filing of insurance claims, revision of procedures, or administrative action to improve the performance of personnel.

(i) Study of Internal Control System

A. *Scope*—The study to be made as the basis for the evaluation of internal control includes two phases: (a) knowledge and understanding of the procedures and methods prescribed and (b) a reasonable degree of assurance that they are in use and are operating as planned. These two phases of study are referred to as the review of the system and tests of compliance, respectively. Although these phases are discussed separately, they are closely related in that some portions of each may be performed concurrently and may contribute to the auditor's evaluation of the prescribed procedures and of the compliance with them.

B. *Review*—The review of the system is primarily a process of obtaining information about the organization and the procedures prescribed and is intended to serve as the basis for test of compliance and for evaluation of the system. The information required for this purpose ordinarily is obtained through discussion with appropriate client/auditee personnel and reference to documentation such as procedure manuals, job descriptions, flowcharts, and decision tables.*

---

*Standards for the Professional Practice of Internal Auditing by The Institute of Internal Auditors, copyright 1978 by The Institute of Internal Auditors, Inc., 290 Maitland Avenue, Altamonte Springs, Florida 32701, U.S.A. Reprinted with permission.

In order to clarify their understanding of information obtained from such sources, some auditors follow the practice of tracing one or a few of the different types of transactions involved through the related documents and records maintained. Information concerning the system may be recorded by the auditor in the form of answers to an internal control questionnaire, narrative memoranda, flowcharts, decision tables, or any other forms that suits the auditor's needs or preferences.

In preparing internal control evaluation guides, all "no" answers must be evaluated by the auditor. There must be a compensation control or the auditor should prepare a tentative recommendation worksheet. A compensating control exists when the lack of a given control does not increase the risk of an error or defalcation occurring.

Upon completion of the review of the system, the auditor should be able to make a preliminary evaluation assuming satisfactory compliance with the prescribed system.

    C. *Tests of Compliance*—The purpose of compliance testing is to provide reasonable assurance that accounting control procedures are being applied as prescribed. Such tests are necessary if the prescribed procedures are to be relied upon in determining the nature, timing, or extent of substantive tests of particular classes of transactions or balances, but are not necessary if the procedures are not to be relied upon for that purpose. The auditor may decide not to rely on the prescribed procedures because he concludes either (a) that the procedures are not satisfactory for that purpose or (b) that the audit effort required to test compliance with the procedures to justify reliance on them in making substantive tests would exceed the reduction in effort that could be achieved by such reliance. The latter conclusion may result from consideration of the nature or amount of the transactions or balances involved, the data processing methods being used, and the auditing procedures that can be applied in making substantive tests.

        1. *Nature of Tests*—Accounting control requires not only that certain procedures be performed but that they be performed properly and independently. Tests of compliance, therefore, are concerned primarily with these questions: Were the necessary procedures performed, how were they performed, were they performed properly, and by whom were they performed?*

Some aspects of accounting control require procedures that are not necessarily required for the execution of transactions. This class of procedures includes the approval or checking of documents evidencing transactions. Tests of such procedures require inspection of the related documents to obtain evidence in the form of signatures, initials, audit stamps, and the like to indicate whether and by whom they were performed and to permit an evaluation of the propriety of their performance.

---

*Standards for the Professional Practice of Internal Auditing by The Institute of Internal Auditors, copyright 1978 by The Institute of Internal Auditors, Inc., 290 Maitland Avenue, Altamonte Springs, Florida 32701, U.S.A. Reprinted with permission.

Other aspects of accounting control require a segregation of duties so that certain procedures are performed independently. The performance of these procedures is largely self-evident from the operation of the business or the existence of its essential records; consequently, tests of compliance with such procedures are primarily for the purpose of determining whether they were performed by persons having no incompatible functions. Examples of this class of procedures may include the receiving, depositing, and disbursing of cash, the recording of transactions, and the posting of customers' accounts. Since such procedures frequently leave no audit trail of documentary evidence as to who performed them, tests of compliance in these situations necessarily are limited to inquiries of different personnel and observation of office personnel and routines to corroborate the information obtained during the initial review of the system. Although reconciliations, confirmations, or other audit tests performed in accordance with the auditing standard relating to evidential matter may substantiate the accuracy of the underlying records, these tests frequently provide no affirmative evidence of segregation of duties because the records may be accurate even though maintained by persons having incompatible functions.

2. *Timing and Extent of Tests*—The purpose of tests of compliance with accounting control procedures is to provide "a reasonable degree of assurance that they are in use and are operating as planned." What constitutes a "reasonable" degree of assurance is a matter of auditing judgment; the "degree of assurance" necessarily depends on the nature, timing, and extent of the tests and on the results obtained.

Accounting control procedures that leave an audit trail of documentary evidence of compliance should ideally be applied to transactions executed throughout the period under audit. The explanation behind this is the general sampling concept according to which the items to be examined should be selected from the entire set of data to which the resulting conclusions are to be applied. Independent auditors often make such tests during interim work. When this has been done, the application of such tests throughout the remaining period may not be necessary.

Factors to be considered in this respect include: (1) the results of the tests during the interim period; (2) responses to inquiries concerning the remaining period; (3) the length of the remaining period; (4) the nature and amount of the transactions or balances involved; (5) evidence of compliance within the remaining period that may be obtained from substantive tests; and (6) other matters the auditor considers relevant in the circumstances.

Tests of compliance may be applied on either a subjective or statistical basis. Statistical sampling may be a practical means for expressing in quantitative terms the auditor's judgment concerning reasonableness and for determining sample size and evaluating sample results on that basis.

(ii) Evaluation of System
A conceptually logical approach to the auditor's evaluation of accounting control, which focuses directly on the purpose of preventing or detecting material errors and irregularities in financial

statements, is to apply the following steps in considering each significant class of transactions and related assets involved in the audit:

- Consider types of errors and irregularities that could occur.

- Determine the accounting control procedures that should prevent or detect such errors and irregularities.

- Determine whether the necessary procedures are prescribed and are being followed satisfactorily.

- Evaluate any weaknesses, that is, types of potential errors and irregularities not covered by existing control procedures, to determine their effect on (1) the nature, timing, or extent of auditing procedures to be applied and (2) suggestions to be made to the client/auditee.

In the practical application of the foregoing approach, the first two steps are performed primarily through the development of questionnaires, checklists, instructions, or similar generalized material used by the auditor. However, professional judgment is required in interpreting, adapting, or expanding such generalized material as appropriate in particular situations. For example, lack of controls as identified on an internal control questionnaire may be mitigated by compensating controls. The third step is accomplished through the review of the system and tests of compliance and the final step through the exercise of professional judgment in evaluating the information obtained in the preceding steps.

The auditor's evaluation of accounting control with reference to each significant class of transactions and related assets should be a conclusion as to whether the prescribed procedures and compliance therewith are satisfactory for his purpose. The procedures and compliance should be considered satisfactory if the auditor's review and test disclose no condition he believes to be a material weakness for his purpose. In this context, a material weakness means a condition in which the auditor believes the prescribed procedures or the degree of compliance with them does not provide reasonable assurance that errors or irregularities in amounts that would be material in the financial statements being audited would be prevented or detected within a timely period by employees in the normal course of performing their assigned functions. These criteria may be broader than those that may be appropriate for evaluating weaknesses in accounting control for management or other purposes.

(iii)   Correlation with Other Auditing Procedures
The timing and extent of other auditing procedures is dependent upon the review and evaluation of the system of internal controls.

The controls of a system can be summarized as nonexistent, excellent, or some combination thereof.

SAM POLE COMPANY	(LOGO)	CORPORATE AUDIT DEPARTMENT	
		PROCEDURES MANUAL	DATE:

TITLE: Evaluating Internal Controls	NO: 2.2	PAGES:

When the controls are nonexistent, the system of controls will not be tested; accordingly, alternate audit procedures will be required.

If the controls are excellent, compliance tests can be performed to verify their excellence. The test will normally cover the period under audit and based upon the results obtained will either limit or modify substantive tests. Substantive tests will be limited when the results confirm our preliminary evaluation, whereas, substantive tests will be modified when errors, (i.e., controls are not functioning properly) are found during the performance of our testing procedures.

The extent of tests required to constitute sufficient evidential matter should vary inversely with the auditor's reliance on internal control. The auditing procedures should provide a reasonable basis for an opinion in all cases, although the portion of reliance derived from the respective sources may vary between cases.

2.3 MATERIALITY

A significant function of auditing is to express an opinion regarding the fairness of financial statements and the adequacy of the system of internal controls or other audited areas. In forming this opinion, judgment must be exercised involving the materiality of exceptions to mathematical accuracy, auditing procedures, compliance with GAAP principles and consistency in the application of those principles.

In their pronouncements, both the American Institute of Certified Public Accountants (AICPA) and the Securities and Exchange Commission (SEC) stress materiality. Bulletins of committees of the AICPA relating to accounting and auditing procedure remind readers that they apply only to "items material and significant in the relative circumstances" and that "items of little or no consequence may be dealt with as expediency may suggest."

Regulations of the SEC require that the accountant express an opinion as to "any material differences between the accounting principles and practices reflected in the financial statements and those reflected in the accounts."

How is the auditor to determine what is material, significant, or of consequence? The courts and the SEC have furnished a few guides, including the following:

A. Where a misrepresentation would be likely to affect the conduct of a reasonable man with reference to a transaction with another person, the misrepresentation is material. (Restatement of the Law of Contracts)

B. A material fact . . . (is) a fact which if it had been correctly stated or disclosed would have deterred or tended to deter the average prudent investor from purchasing the securities in question. (Securities and Exchange Commission. In Matter of Howard, et al., 1 SEC 6)

C. The term "material," when used to qualify a requirement for the furnishing of information as to any subject, limits the information required to those matters as to which an average prudent investor ought reasonably to be informed before purchasing the security registered. (Securities and Exchange Commission, Regulation C, Rule 405, of Securities Act Regulations)

From these definitions we may conclude that materiality depends upon surrounding circumstances, the setting in which the item appears, and the setting in which it will be used. If the probable effect of the item—whether through omission or commission—would be to give rise to misleading inferences by the person or class of persons whom it will logically reach, it is material, significant, consequential, and important. For this purpose these four words are practically synonymous, although some make a distinction between material and significant, attaching material primarily to dollar amount.

Clearly there are degrees of materiality and as a consequence there will be borderline cases. These will require all the good judgment which the auditor can summon.

Standards which would guide an auditor in determining whether or not a deviation would require correction, disclosure, or qualification of an opinion would be of immense help to auditors.

Research shows that the assessment of materiality differs among individual accountants and among public accounting firms and that it varies with the size and geographical location of the practice. In arriving at his decisions, these are some of the matters the auditor should bear in mind:

- *Relative size of the item*—Failure to disclose a liability of $5,000 in the balance sheet of an enterprise with net assets of $30,000 would result in a material misstatement. In a balance sheet showing net assets of $3,000,000 it would ordinarily not be material.

- *Absolute size*—In spite of the importance of relativity, size alone may be important. Many accountants would consider a large amount important, even though it is only 3 or 4 percent of net assets or 3 or 4 percent of net income before taxes.

- *The nature of disclosure*—The fact that a company has pledged its accounts receivable as security for a loan is significant because it discloses that the company is using a comparatively expensive form of financing and is therefore a material fact even though the amount may not be material in relation to the working capital.

- *Use to be made of the report*—If it is known that the report will be used for the sale of stock or for obtaining long- or short-term credit, the effect the item might have on purchasers or long- or short-term creditors would be considered.

- *Evidence of a desire to mislead*—The existence of an incentive for error would be considered. An accidental error would have less significance than a deliberate departure from accepted procedure.

- *The favorable or unfavorable effect of adjustment or disclosure*—Unfavorable ones are usually given more weight.

- *Stability of income*—If net pre-tax income fluctuates widely, unusual items are more important.

- *Effect on future earnings*—Items whose effect will continue into the future are more important than those of only current significance.

Materiality may determine not only the need for exception or disclosure but the extent of the audit work necessary to sustain an informed opinion. Inventories of a manufacturing company are of greater relative importance than those of a personal service organization, not only in size and amount but because of the greater number of ways in which they may be improperly handled, both physically and in the records. Where accounts receivable consist of relatively few, but large, balances, the percentage of accounts confirmed should normally be much higher than if they comprise a large number of small balances, even though the total may be the same.

In summary, sound judgment is required in determining what is or is not material. No definition of materiality need deter you from recommending adjustments of errors or omissions on the books or financial statements. Auditees, as mentioned earlier, generally wish to have errors or deficiencies corrected.

2.4 TYPES OF AUDITS

The following descriptions are of the audit types performed by the Internal Audit Department. The majority of audits performed by the department are financial, operational/managerial, and EDP. (For a discussion of Control Self Assessment (CSA) or Self Audits see Section 1.1 (e).)The type of audit performed on a particular auditable unit can be any combination of the types described below. The type of audit to be performed is determined in the initial planning process.

(a) High-Level Review of Procedures

A high-level review is a special type of review that measures general compliance with key corporate policies and with sound business practices. The objectives of this review are to provide the auditor with an understanding of an operation and to determine the nature of detailed testing that may be needed in certain areas.

Procedures for this review follow the general guidelines for external auditors, as specified in "Statement on Auditing Standards No. 36: Review of Interim Financial Information." These procedures consist primarily of inquiries and analytical review concerning significant accounting matters relating to financial information being reviewed. Additionally, the internal auditor should obtain an understanding of the entity's systems of accounting and internal controls.

Our high level review includes other tests outlined in greater detail than in SAS 36. Compliance and some substantive tests are to be performed over certain areas of an entity; including cash, accounts receivable, credit, travel and expense, brand sales, product costing, marketing variable, fixed assets, debts, and inventory.

(b) Financial Audit

A financial audit is a study of the current financial position of an operation to evaluate the fair presentation of the financial position as reported in the balance sheet, income statement, and the statement of cash flows. Full financial audits of significant company operations and subsidiaries are typically performed by external, independent auditors. However in some cases, full financial audits may be performed by Sam Pole's internal auditors.

The primary reason for a financial audit is to assure parties relying on financial statements that the data is presented fairly in accordance with GAAP. A financial audit would be appropriate before tax reporting, expansion ventures, mergers, acquisitions, disposal, economy fluctuations, and periodic presentations of financial position.

The approach to a financial audit would be governed by the purpose of the audit. If current liquidity were of prime importance, collectibility of trade receivables, short-term investments, turnover of inventory and liquidation of accounts payable would be considered. If expansion or acquisition were of prime importance, both long- and short-term debt would be considered. If economic fluctuations called for entrenchment, then purchasing practices, inventory stockpiling, overhead reductions, and other operating costs would be considered. Regardless of the purpose of the audit, financial controls would always be of prime consideration in evaluating audit risk.

In all financial audits, the general ledger, general and special journals, voucher registers, bank reconciliation and account analyses would be reviewed. These records would tell us where the operation's assets were utilized and why. Depending on the purpose of the audit, a review of the following reports would be considered:

- Accounts Receivable Aging

- Accounts Payable Aging

- Inventory Aging

- Discount Income versus Discount Expense

- Physical Inventory Reconciliations

- Inventory/Receivable Turnover Ratios

- Variance Analyses

- Standard Cost Revisions

- Transportation Costs

- Capital Expenditures versus Return on Investments

- Purchasing Cost Savings.

These records and reports would tell the auditor where the operation was, where it has gone, and how it got there. They would highlight efficiencies and inefficiencies in vital areas such as credit and collections, inventory control, production scheduling, capital investments, and purchasing coordination.

Given all the above factors, the audit plan would then be devised, giving consideration to:

- Objective of the audit

- Time requirements

- Staff requirements

- Starting and concluding dates

- Auditor assignments.

(c) Operational/Managerial Audit

An operational audit can be defined as an extension of a financial audit. A financial audit tells you where you were and where you are; an operational audit tends to answer the questions why you are where you are and how you got there. In this sense, the operational audit falls into the category of a management service by evaluating the four functions of management: (1) planning, (2) organizing, (3) directing and (4) controlling. The operational audit can be broken down further as a functional review, i.e. Purchasing as a department versus the overall Procurement operation in coordination with Production Scheduling and Market Forecasting. Several reasons for performing an operational audit are compliance with policies and procedures, excessive customer returns, equipment down time, adverse variances, proposed product changes, thefts, or personnel turnover. The timeliness of an operational audit is determined by the reason for the audit and the areas to be audited.

To formulate the approach to an operational audit, an auditor must first establish the scope. This step determines the extent of the audit. The next step is to become familiar with an auditee's operation, its purpose in the total structure of the entity, its history, its staff, and its reporting path. The reporting path is of prime importance because this is the communication route along which audit results and conclusions will flow. The auditor should advise the location's management (in advance) of his planned visit so that suitable working and living accommodations may be arranged.

The prime records to be obtained in an operational audit are the organization chart of the function/operation, applicable policy guides, and procedures directives. These will outline each employee's responsibility and authority. The functions/operation's performance reports for at least one year prior to the audit should be reviewed to determine trends which have developed over the past year. These records and reports could indicate such trouble areas as segregation of duties, imbalance in reporting path, over- or under staffing, noncompliance with corporate policies and procedures, weaknesses in internal controls, or inadequate job rotations. These indications could aid the auditor in determining priorities as to depth of investigation and areas of potential improvement. Reports must be informative and timely, and directed to the proper levels of management.

(d) Compliance Audit

A compliance audit involves two different, though closely related, types of issues:

- The nature and scope of the transaction against which the compliance is to be ascertained

- The degree to which it is practicable, or even desirable, to determine the compliance.

Therefore, a compliance audit can be defined as a rerun of a given task over a prescribed course which is monitored by various checkpoints to reach a desired conclusion.

Reasons for a compliance audit can vary with the size and complexity of the organization, type of product, market involvement, quantity and locations of sites or levels of standardization. A compliance audit may be performed due to a recent history of excess customer returns, unusual buildup of inventory, increase in scrap, increase in bad debt write-offs, proposed realignment of responsibilities, manpower turnover, or a routine review of procedures.

The basic records reviewed in performing a compliance audit are applicable operations manuals and procedure guidelines. Some typical reports to be reviewed are purchase orders issued, comparative scrap levels, comparative quantities of customer returns, and equipment maintenance hours. From a review of these records and reports and adequate testing of the procedures, the auditor should be able to conclude on the level or quality of compliance and on the existence of proper procedures.

(e) Contract Audit

A contract audit is defined as the review and evaluation of a contract (terms, conditions, etc.) and its related financial transactions. The terms construction and contracts are sometimes used interchangeably in the audit profession because a construction project requires a contract. However, contracts cover a wide range of areas such as repairs, maintenance, rentals, and consulting.

Contract Audit Objectives are segregated into:

Corporate Audit Objectives:

- Assess the adequacy of internal accounting control systems and operating procedures

- Monitor compliance with corporate policies and procedures, contractual provisions, budgetary guidelines, and operating safeguards and controls

- Highlight problem/opportunity areas and make appropriate recommendations to management for the development of new operating and control procedures.

Contract Audit Objectives:

- The contract specifically includes the right to audit clause

- Controls exist to assure that construction or other costs, which are billed by the contractor, are in accordance with the terms of the contract

- Contractor controls and procedures are adequate to assure that the billed costs are proper and reasonable

- Controls exist to assure that other charges to the project are proper and reasonable.

Contract audits are appropriate on a continuing basis when:

- Contracts are issued for significant amounts

- Actual expenditures exceed budget

- Control weaknesses are noted during a financial audit
- A unit experiences management turnover
- Integrity of personnel is questioned
- A request is received from management (corporate or unit).

The approach to a contract audit includes the following steps:

- Review the contract to determine that it is in accordance with established company policies (e.g. competitive bidding)
- Document and evaluate the system of internal control
- Review pertinent data (project expenditures) to determine test criteria
- Perform a review to ascertain that all expenditures (included in test) are accurate, properly supported, and in agreement with terms and conditions of contract
- If considered necessary, visit the contractor's office and review records to determine that charges to the company are proper.

Ongoing contract audits require the preparation of periodic interim reports to management advising on situations encountered so that prompt corrective action can be taken. A formal report is also required upon completion of an assignment, and status reports to audit management should also be issued from time to time.

(f) Desk Review

The internal auditor will obtain a package of financial and other documentary information from the auditee and perform limited procedures. In most cases, all procedures will be performed from corporate offices and not at the auditee location.

Several benefits result from frequent desk reviews. The internal auditor can determine if previous recommendations to the auditee are currently complied with. The internal auditor can expand the coverage of his audits to nearly the entire organization without making trips to every location. A related benefit is reduced travel time and travel expenses. Finally, the desk review is ideal for training new internal auditors, allowing them to gain understanding of an entity's operations prior to doing a field audit.

(g) Follow-Up Audits

Follow-up audits are performed six to twelve months after a major audit has been completed, to ensure that previously accepted audit recommendations have been effectively implemented. These audits are typically performed if the audit identified significant conditions.

(h) EDP Audits

EDP Audits are the examination of significant aspects of the electronic data processing environment. The company may have several different EDP environments, such as: mainframe or mini- or microcomputers—including Local Area and/or Wide Area Networks (LANs or WANs). Each environment should be considered separately as an EDP Audit.

In addition, each environment should have identified audit units. The following is a list of major audit units to be considered for each environment but the list may not be fully inclusive:

- *General Controls Review*—Review of organizational structure policies regarding documentation standards, access security, program change control and continuity of operations. This could be done in conjunction with other audits (Integrated Approach).

- *Detailed Controls Review/Audit*—Examination of general control systems such as:
  - Access security—"TopSecret," RAC-F, ACF-2
  - Program change control—"PanValet"
  - Disaster Recovery

- *Financial Application Controls Review*—Examination of software systems processing applications such as:
  - Accounts receivable
  - General ledger

- *Detailed Examination of Operating System*—Audit specific to MVS operating system, AS/400 or Novell/DOS.

(i) International Audits

An International Audit is a full-scope audit of a particular division or subsidiary. These are performed on a regular basis or on request. The scope of this type of audit includes a financial section, an operational section, an EDP section, and a section addressing the unique characteristics of the location's customs and duties and governmental affairs.

2.5 TIME REPORTING

Planning and budgeting are important procedures that should be performed as integral elements of every audit. Time records aid these functions because they provide cumulative data regarding the actual time spent accomplishing specific assignments on previous or similar engagements. As a result, the senior auditor can use this data, along with an evaluation of the procedures to be performed and the capabilities of the applicable personnel in order to better estimate (budget) the time required for the current audit.

Other benefits of time reporting are:

- *Providing the quantitative support necessary at the staff level*—Accurate budgeting of all audit activities throughout the year will summarize into a viable total from which to determine the number of auditors required.

- *Adding to job control*—Prompt time reporting enables the in-charge to effectively analyze how much time has been spent, how matters stand against the budget, and how much further time is required for completion.

- *Supporting productivity*—Time reporting provides the ability to monitor actual time spent on audits versus administrative and other lost productive time.

The following discussion is an explanation of a basic time reporting form as well as a listing of basic reports. Each audit assignment should be given a number indicating the year and audit number—beginning with 001, followed by 002, etc. Task and audit type codes should be added as described below.

(a) Form: Corporate Audit Time Report

A form is to be completed semimonthly and approved by the senior, supervising senior, or manager. A sample of this form is provided at the end of this section (Figure 2.4).

General Instructions for Completing The Corporate Audit Time Summary

1. Complete form in detail. Be neat.

2. Account for eight hours per day and forty hours per week.

3. Corporate Audit time reports are due semimonthly.

4. Record time accurately to within one-half hour.

(b)   Report for the Period Ending

The form is designed to be used for either the first through the fifteenth, or the sixteenth through the thirty-first of the month.

(c)   Auditor's Name/Employee Number

The auditor to whom the time report pertains should sign the time report. Each auditor should have been assigned an employee number for time reporting purposes.

(d)   Job Number

Each assignment will have a specific job number. Job numbers assist in the identification and accumulation of time reported by several individuals on various jobs. If you are asked to perform a task, obtain the appropriate job number from your supervisor or get the number from the planning memo in the administrative binder for that job.

(e)   Audit Codes

Audit codes relate to the type of audit. A listing of these and task codes appears at the end of this section (Figure 2.3).

(f)   Task Codes

Task codes should be used to detail the specific work performed. A listing of these codes appears at the end of this section (Figure 2.3). If you are unsure of the proper task code, consult your supervisor or the job budget in the planning memo.

(g)   Hours

Only total hours for the semimonthly period need to be recorded in the "hours" column. The daily hours are accumulated on the right side of the sheet. Hours should be reported to the half hour.

(h)   Productive Time

Record *all* time applicable to the job. This includes time spent working at the job site, in the office at night, in the motel, or at home. Think of reporting time as though you were going to bill your time to the auditee. Remember, future projects will be understated if hidden times are not recorded. Record travel as work time only between the normal work hours of 8:00 A.M. and 5:00 P.M., or normal hours for a four-day week. This should be charged to the normal job number, audit code, and task 24.

SAM POLE COMPANY

(LOGO)

CORPORATE AUDIT DEPARTMENT

PROCEDURES MANUAL

DATE:

TITLE: Time Reporting

NO: 2.5

PAGES:

Figure 2.3   Time System Codes: Audit Type Codes and Task Codes

Audit Type Codes
01	High-Level Review
02	Financial Audit
03	Operational Audit
04	EDP Audit
05	Contract Audit
06	Other Audit
99	Nonaudit

Task Codes

01	Planning/Planning Memo	40	Preimplementation System Review
02	Audit Program/ICEG Development	41	Postimplementation System Review
03	Technical Research	42	Systems—Operational
04	Supervision	50	Contract Review
05	Review Workpapers	51	Contract Procedures/Controls
06	Write Reports/Memos	52	Contract Billing
07	General	53	Investigation
08	Cash	54	Benefit Plans
09	A/R Confirmation	55	Projects*
10	Inventories/Physical Obs.	60	Quality Control
11	Supplies Inventory	61	Performance Evaluation
12	Inventories—G/L	62	Orientation
13	Other Assets	63	Scheduling
14	Liabilities	64	Interviewing/Recruiting
15	Revenue/Expense	65	Education and Training Administration
16	Payroll	66	Administrative—Other*
17	Revenue System—Cycle	70	Staff Training—Internal
18	Payment System—Cycle	71	Conferences/Seminars
19	Payroll System—Cycle	72	Education Course—CPE
20	Production System—Cycle	73	Professional Organization
21	Auditee Conferences	74	Self Study
22	Permanent Files	75	Time Report Input
23	System Files	80	Sick
24	Travel—Work Time	81	Personal
25	Travel—Other	82	Vacation
		83	Holiday
30	Data Center Review	84	Compensation
31	Applications Review	90	Administrative—Department*
32	Production/Maintenance	91	Peer Review
33	Computer Program Changes	92	Status Reports
34	Conversions	99	Other
35	EDP Operating System		

*Details to be listed on back of time report

Figure 2.4 Sample Corporate Audit Time Summary Form

SAMPLE
CORPORATE AUDIT DEPARTMENT

NAME: **JOHN DOE**　　EMP. NO.: **450**　　PAGE **1** OF **1**

TIME SUMMARY – PERIOD ENDING **3/15/92**　　REVIEWED BY _____

JOB	AUDIT	TASK	HOURS	DELETE	16	17	20	21	22	23	24	27	28	29	30	DESCRIPTION
000	99	92	3.0	☐						1					2	Admin.-Time Share / Exp. Report
005	01	08	24.0	☐	8	8	8									Cash
005	01	24	5.0	☐				5								Travel Work Time
005	99	25	5.0	☐							5					Travel Nonwork
005	01	09	26.0	☐				3	8	7	8					Accounts Receivable
000	99	80	8.0	☐								8				Sick
010	03	32	22.0	☐									8	8	6	CAAPs Development
					8	**8**	**8**	**8**	**8**	**8**	**13**	**8**	**8**	**8**	**8**	TOTALS

TOTALS 93.0

(i) Nonproductive Time

Record travel time outside normal working hours of 8:00 A.M. to 5:00 P.M., Monday through Friday or after a forty-hour week of flexible hours have been worked. An example is to assume you left the job at 4:00 P.M. after you have spent seven hours on the audit at the job site. One hour should be recorded as productive time and the remainder of the time spent traveling should be recorded as nonproductive.

Travel time is defined as the time required to commute to the airport, from departure airport to airport destination, and the commute from destination airport to office, home, or motel. If you are traveling by automobile, it is that time you leave the home, office, job site, etc., until you arrive at your destination. Travel during nonwork hours should be charged to the job number, audit code 99, and task 25.

Other nonproductive time, including vacation, holidays, sick, personal, training, and seminars, have specific task codes that are self-explanatory. Time charged to the administrative category must be explained on the back of the time report to avoid making it a catch-all task code. All non-productive charges go to job number 000 audit code 99 with the appropriate task.

Administrative is defined as work which is beneficial to all jobs, not just one. If you are writing the report for job number 91-010 in the office, it would be chargeable to job number 91-010. But, if you are writing a policy statement which applies to office procedure and would affect the conduct of all jobs, then the hours would be charged to administrative. We would normally expect very little staff time charged to the administrative category. As a general rule, all staff time should be charged to a job. However, time spent filling out time reports, expense reports, etc., should be considered administrative.

(j) Summarizing Time

Each individual's time is entered into a time reporting application after it has been approved. Once all time sheets are input, the data is compiled into various reports by the application. The following reports should be considered:

Report 10 —Listing of employee names and numbers
Report 20 —Listing of job numbers and job names
Report 30 —Listing of audit numbers and names
Report 40 —Listing of task numbers and task names
Report 50 —Semimonthly input summarized by employee number within date
Report 60 —Listing of hours by job number, employee, and task
Report 70 —Listing of hours by employee, by job, and by task
Report 80 —Listing of hours by audit, by job, employee, and task
Report 90 —Listing of total audit and nonaudit hours by employee
Report 100—Listing of nonaudit hours by employee, by task
Report 110—Listing of budgeted versus actual hours by job, by task
Report 120—Listing of budget to actual hours for all jobs

2.6 EXPENSE REPORTING

All approved expense reports should be submitted to the Audit Director. A copy should be retained for the department's records. This will provide a means for assisting us in reconciling our monthly "Departmental Budget Progress Reports" on a timely basis, and will provide you with a record, if necessary.

(a) Travel Expenses

General guidelines for travel arrangements and travel expenses:

- *Airfare*—Flight arrangements should be made through the travel department in accordance with corporate policy.

- *Lodging*—Lodging arrangements are to be made through the travel department but are first to be approved by the manager level or above.

- *Meals*—Reasonable meal expenses will be reimbursed.

- *Local Transportation*—The decision of whether to lease a car or use cabs is to be discussed at the manager level or above. Car rental is to be arranged through the travel department.

- *Telephone*—Nonexcessive expenses for personal calls will be reimbursed however personal calls should be limited to one per day.

- *Advances*—Expense advances are to be obtained through the accounting department and are to be approved by the manager level or above.

- *Expense Report Settlements*—Individual auditors are responsible for settling their own expense reports with the accounting department.

- *Mileage*—Mileage expenses will be reimbursed at the current rate acceptable to the Internal Revenue Service.

This list serves only a general guideline and exceptions will occur; however, you will be asked to explain deviations. When in doubt, the general company guidelines apply. Before leaving on a trip, any expected exceptions must be discussed at the manager or director level.

Chapter 3

AUDIT PERFORMANCE

3.1 CORPORATE AUDIT PERFORMANCE PROCESS MATRIX
    (a) Assignment Log and Checklist
        (i) Audit Performance Process Log
    (b) Description of Notice to Auditee
    (c) Preliminary Survey
        (i) Purpose
        (ii) Progression of and Procedures for Preliminary Survey
    (d) Planning Memo
        (i) Purpose
        (ii) Objective
        (iii) Procedure
        (iv) Format
    (e) Audit Status Report
    (f) Developing Audit Recommendations
        (i) Recommendation Worksheet
        (ii) Form Format

3.2 WORKPAPERS
    (a) Control
    (b) Retention
    (c) Headings
    (d) Permanent Files—Contents and Format
    (e) Current Files—Contents and Format
    (f) General Organization
    (g) Detailed Workpaper Section Organization
    (h) Indexing and Cross Referencing
    (i) Referencing
    (j) Standard Tick Marks

3.3 AUDIT OBJECTIVES

3.1 CORPORATE AUDIT PERFORMANCE PROCESS MATRIX

The audit process ranges from the notification of the auditee and staff through the performance evaluation of each staff on the project. The corporate audit performance matrix (Figure 3.1) summarizes the activities contained within our sample audit process. This sample process places a heavy emphasis on organization and implementation of all authorized department procedures. It is a structured program with a great deal of attention to planning. The importance of structuring the audit process and following documented department procedures cannot be over emphasized. It is through the strict adherence to procedures performed by competent staff that good audit reports will result.

The example included in this Manual requires the audit team to formally notify the auditee and develop a detailed audit plan and budget. The purpose of the detailed audit plan is to ensure that the objectives of the audit are the most appropriate for the circumstances. Given the limitation of time for each audit, the scope and objectives should be seriously considered not only by field staff auditors, but by the audit management. This process is institutionalized through the development of a proper audit planning document.

The budget will help guide the staff to put their time into the proper areas. It will also assist audit management in explaining why audits have taken more or less time than originally planned. Budgets also help refine the long-term planning process and provide improved credibility for the audit function. One must always keep in mind that it is very difficult to measure audit productivity. With budgets in place, some of the management and auditee doubts are mitigated.

(a) Assignment Log and Checklist

At the commencement of an audit assignment, a number is given to the audit project. The number consists of two digits for the year and a three-digit number designating this particular engagement.

One of the first steps in the audit performance process is to initiate an assignment checklist. (See Figure 3.2). The Assignment Checklist is used as an overall control form and should be the first paper seen on the top of a workpaper binder set. This checklist is a guide to insure that all critical elements of the audit performance process are completed.

(i) Audit Performance Process Log
In order to maintain control over all audit assignments, a log is kept by the Department Administrator. The log consists of a column to the left indicating the year and audit number. These are followed by columns to the right indicating the status of the audit and the beginning of the report initiation and completion process.

(b) Description of Notice to Auditee

As discussed in Section 3.1, in our example, we have opted to notify auditees in advance of audits. In some cases, this may not be appropriate. For instance, petty cash counts are usually performed on a

Figure 3.1 Corporate Audit Performance Process Matrix

	ASSIGNMENT CHECK LIST —	ENGAGEMENT MEMO — NOTICE TO AUDITEE [SECTION 3.2]	PLANNING MEMO	STATUS MEMO	TENTATIVE AUDIT RECOMMENDATIONS WORKSHEET	AUDIT REPORT DISTRIBUTION WORKSHEET	AUDIT REPORT [SEE SECTION 4.1—REPORT PROCESS]	SUMMARY MEMO	PERFORMANCE EVALUATIONS
PURPOSE	Establish control over audit *Assign number and log*	Announce audit	Establish audit objective, scope, and approach	Interim field audit report of significant findings/problems	Document significant findings	Track report preparation and issuance	Document results of audit reported to Audit Committee	Document achieved audit objectives; budget/actual time comparison	Periodic evaluation of performance on engagement
TIMING	Begin two weeks before audit; complete one week after report is issued	Approximately four weeks before audit	Before or at beginning of audit	As required, based upon existing circumstances	Promptly upon audit disclosure	Upon completion of field work	One week after Manager approval of agreed text	Promptly upon completion of final draft of audit report	To accompany Summary Memo
AUTHOR ADDRESSEE COPIES	Senior Workpapers None	I.A. Manager Unit Head Unit Controller, Manager, others	Senior I.A. Manager Manager	Senior I.A. Manager Manager	Auditor Auditee workpapers	Senior/Manager Workpapers None	I.A. Manager Audit Committee Distribution to Management	Senior I.A. Manager	I.A. Manager Staff Personnel
CONTENTS	Calendar of audit checkpoints	Audit entity or location, audit objectives, audit period start date, end date, request response	Audit objective, audit scope timing, budget hours detailed by area, significant audit areas/audit, approach staffing	Outline of significant audit developments, timing problems, need to alter objective or scope, high-level budget/actual hours comparison	Findings documentation, status and disposition	Calendar of checkpoints; distribution of copies	ID of audit transmittal to Audit Committee, highlights of audited entity, scope of audit, auditors' conclusions, detailed comments and recommendations (for management only)	Outline achieved audit objectives or shortcomings, detailed budget/ actual hours comparison with explanations, future audit recommendations, oral report to director of significant findings before audit report	As prescribed on form
APPROVAL	None	None	Manager	None	Senior	Manager	None	Manager	

102

Figure 3.2   Sam Pole Company Corporate Audit Department Assignment Checklist

Audit #93—XXX

COMPANY: _____
LOCATION: _____
ASSIGNMENT: _____
DATE: _____

Date

1. Notice to Auditee _____
2. Planning Memo _____
3. Field Work
      Preaudit Conference _____
      Begun _____
      Status Memo _____
      Completed _____
4. Closing Conference _____
5. Senior finalization of workpapers _____
6. Manager review (two days before outside deadlines) _____
7. Audit Report draft _____
8. Summary Memo _____
9. Audit Report issued _____
10. Performance Evaluations _____

Name   Completed by Date

Supervising: _____   _____
In Charge: _____   _____
Assistant: _____   _____

surprise basis. However, in general circumstances, we believe it is more appropriate to notify the auditee that an audit will take place. This allows for an orderly project.

Some audit departments do not choose this approach because the auditee can improve or address areas that may be audited. We believe that if the notice of audit provides the impetus for the auditee department to improve, that is accomplishing the spirit of the audit mission. What follows in Figure 3.3 is a sample notice to auditee. The Manual should contain a sample so that there is a consistency within the audit practice.

(c) Preliminary Survey

(i) Purpose

The purpose of a preliminary survey is to:

- Gain a basic understanding of the entity to be audited

- Begin the planning process.

Both purposes relate to generally accepted auditing standards and "Standards for the Professional Practice of Internal Auditing." The first general standard states that: "The examination is to be performed by a person or persons having adequate technical training and proficiency as an auditor. "The first standard of field work states that: "The work is to be adequately planned and assistants, if any, are to be properly supervised."

According to the IIA standards for the Professional Practice of Internal Auditing (SPPIA), item 410 Planning and Audit, auditors should obtain background information about the activities to be audited. This is accomplished by performing, as appropriate, an on-site survey to become familiar with activities and controls to be audited, to identify areas for audit emphasis, and to invite comments and suggestions.

To perform an audit in accordance with generally accepted auditing standards and IIA-SSPIA, a properly conducted preliminary survey is required.

(ii) Progression of and Procedures for Preliminary Survey

Review the scope of the pending audit.

The comprehensiveness of the survey depends on the scope of audit. For example, if the audit is limited in scope, then the survey will be limited. A memo should be prepared discussing the following:

- Purpose of the engagement

- Nature of the final report, if any

Figure 3.3   Sample Notice to Auditee

September 10, 199x

Mr. E. S. Jones
Sam Pole Company
2010 Main Street
Anytown, USA

Dear Mr. Jones:

In accordance with our audit plan, we have scheduled an audit during the period from September 1 through September 9, 19xx. It will be performed under the supervision of Mr. Justin Tyme who will arrive in the office on September 1.

A full financial audit will be conducted including the evaluation of internal controls and tests of transactions supporting related account balances as well as verification of physical inventory valuations and circulation of customer accounts receivable balances.

Please contact me if you have any questions related to our visit or if you have areas of concern that you may wish to have reviewed.

Very truly yours,

Newley A. Pointed
Audit Manager

- Timing of the engagement
- Auditee contacts.

Arrange a preliminary meeting with management.

The purposes of this meeting are to:

- Meet management and inform them of the objectives of the survey
- Arrange for working space
- Prepare preliminary time tables
- Gain the confidence of location management
- Gain an understanding of management's objectives
- Gain understanding of problems as perceived by local management.

Write a memo documenting the preliminary meeting with management. The following should be included in the memo:

- Time, date, and participation (who was there)
- Summary of topics discussed
- All problems noted
- Potential conflicts
- Office policies peculiar to that location.

After a memo is prepared documenting the preliminary meeting with management, the field work portion of the survey is ready to begin.

Preliminary survey field procedures should be conducted.

The field survey procedures for a full scope audit are:

- Through interview, observation and documentation, gain an understanding of the following characteristics of the entity:
  - Brief history of the entity
  - Size of entity

CORPORATE AUDIT DEPARTMENT

PROCEDURES MANUAL		DATE:

TITLE: Performance Process Matrix | NO: 3.1 | PAGES:

- Products produced
- Process flow
- Principal customers
- Principal suppliers
- Current trends.

The understanding should be documented in memorandum form. The purpose is to provide the reader with an overall understanding of the entity as it relates to Sam Pole Company.

- Perform a cursory review of the accounting system by obtaining and preparing the appropriate documents and memoranda:

    - Obtain an organization chart

    - Determine the extent of EDP usage

    - Briefly describe the following systems. Note the volume of transactions and the apparent control points and control weaknesses

        - purchasing, accounts payable and cash disbursements

        - order entry, sales, accounts receivable, and cash receipts

        - metals accounting

        - supply inventory system

        - cost accounting system

        - fixed assets and depreciation

        - general ledger system.

    The following questions should be answered for each system:

        - What is the job?

        - Who does it?

        - Why is it done?

        - How is it done?

        - Where is it done?

        - When is it done?

> – How is it monitored?

> – How much does it cost?

Prepare a schedule of all books of original entry.

Prepare a schedule of primary management reports.

Overview systems flowcharts may be prepared for any of the accounting systems if it enhances the understanding.

- In connection with the review of the accounting system, the following documents should be identified if available:

  - Internal accounting procedures and practice manuals

  - Governmental regulatory reports

  - Prior audit reports, both internal and independent

  - Authoritative accounting publications related to the industry

  - Industry standards.

- Perform a risk analysis: Professional practice standards require the auditor to exercise due professional care. Due professional care is not intended to mean that the auditor is infallible or that extraordinary performance is to be expected. But it does require that reasonable care be taken. In order to exercise due professional care, the auditor must be aware of potential risks.

  A risk can be defined as an exposure to loss or to less than the maximization of efficiency resulting from the lack of internal controls.

  Common risks

  - Inadequate controls

  - Inadequate planning and organizing

  - Inadequate directing and controlling—A cursory internal control review using standard internal control questionnaires is perhaps the easiest and most expedient means to detect common risks. Standard internal control questionnaires will contain questions that point out unique risks for each system under review. An analysis of answers to the forms will aid the auditor in determining: (1) If the nature of the weakness is confined to one system; (2) If the nature of the weakness is pervasive throughout the entire organization.

For example, if the auditor notes a lack of segregation of duties in cash, he/she should determine whether it is unique to cash or pervasive throughout the whole system of internal control. If the weaknesses are pervasive throughout the whole system of internal control, then the problem would be one of inadequate planning and organizing. If the weaknesses are confined only to cash, then the problem would be one of inadequate directing and controlling.

Collation of risks—To assess the effectiveness of internal controls, it is necessary to relate risks to exposure, to controls, to planned audit effort, and then to the eventual results of the audit procedures. A suggested format is to schedule the above on workpapers which will be used during the actual performance of the audit.

Evaluation of risks—Evaluation of risks consists of the auditor's evaluation of the exposure resulting from the lack of functioning of an internal control over the particular risk. It consists of the auditor's answers to the question, "What is the maximum exposure to the corporation if this particular internal control is not functioning?" In answering the question, the auditor must consider any compensating controls that may be in existence. To write an effective audit plan, it will be necessary to identify, relate, and evaluate the risks.

(d) Planning Memo

(i) Purpose

The planning memo outlines the manner in which the department audit plan is to be implemented for a specific audit, special assignment, or other activity. Planning represents an extremely important aspect of auditing and is required by the Institute of Internal Auditors and the AICPA's "Statement of Auditing Standards of Field Work No. 1."

Before each assignment, a planning memo is required to establish coordination between internal audit staff and management. This document will ensure that the objectives and scheduling of the audit are being communicated and understood by all involved. Properly implemented it ensures that the more experienced auditors (management) consider scope and procedures prior to implementation.

(ii) Objective

The planning memo serves several purposes; namely, to document audit objectives, auditee background information, and financial highlights; to describe significant audit procedures, budgeted hours, engagement timing and personnel assigned.

(iii) Procedure

Planning memos are to be typed on interoffice stationery and addressed to the Director of Auditing. A copy is also included in the workpapers.

The planning memo should be completed far enough in advance of an assignment for manager review and approval. Prior to preparing the memo, the senior, if circumstances warrant, may have to visit the audit site to conduct a preliminary survey to obtain sufficient information to complete the planning memo. Only in unusual circumstances will the planning memo be accepted, after the audit has been started. If after the audit begins, conditions change, affecting the initial planning memo, an addendum should be written and forwarded to the manager. The addendum should explain and document the reason for the changes, even if previous telephone approval has been obtained.

(iv) Format

The format, designed to be used on a consistent basis, for a planning memo is shown in Figure 3.4 and a brief explanation for each section appears in the following list:

Introduction—This first brief paragraph outlines what was stated in the "Notice to Auditee" (Section 3.1). It should contain the name and location of the entity to be audited, scheduled dates to begin and complete field work, a brief description of the type of audit, and the audit date(s).

Objective—The deliverable product of an assignment requires a conclusion which will provide management with either assurances or reasons for action concerning, for example, account balances, internal controls, various functions or operational procedures, and so on. Prior to the audit, we must plan to ensure that our objective will direct our efforts toward that end result. Establishing objectives encourages an orderly work process and concentration of the audit effort toward a predefined goal. Consideration should be directed toward potential high risk or material areas.

Scope—Having stated the objective in the previous section, the planning memo logically leads into the scope section. If the objective is to state an opinion on the adequacy of a certain system, then the scope will explain compliance and the substantive testing necessary to arrive at an opinion. Areas of emphasis should be defined along with significant audit steps, and procedures.

Background—Background information is necessary in order to give the reader a description of the entity or area to be audited. It does not need to be long or detailed but should contain the entity name, location and procedures or description of operations. Facts that are unusual or pertinent should be identified. Examples include situations where the controller is new, the location is known to have had internal control problems in the past, sales have fallen off heavily, or operating costs have increased substantially.

Financial Highlights—The financial highlights section includes a summary of major account balances. Accounts outlined in the objective section are also included in order to bring these accounts to the attention of the reader. To further increase the reader's information, comparative figures for two corresponding periods should be included.

Significant Audit Areas/Audit Approach—This section identifies and outlines the more significant areas mentioned in the scope section. It also states the audit approach to be used in these areas.

Figure 3.4   Sample Planning Memo

Date: October 20, 199x
From: Senior
To: Manager
Subject: Planning Memo—Sam Pole's Best Ozone Paint Manufacturing Facility

Field work for the manufacturing facility interim audit will begin on Monday, October 26, 19xx, and will be completed on Friday, November 20, 19xx. The interim audit as of September 30, 19xx, will include a financial audit. A year-end audit will also be performed by the internal audit department in January 19xx.

Objective

The interim audit will be conducted to determine the adequacy of internal accounting controls (through a review of accounting systems and a test of transactions) as a basis for the formulation of year-end balances.

A year-end review will also be conducted to determine the validity of accounting data which will be included in your company's consolidated general ledger trial balance as of December 31, 19xx.

Scope—Interim

The audit will include the documentation, review, and detail compliance testing of existing key internal accounting controls in significant financial areas as of September 30, 19xx, trial balance.

Emphasis will be on inventory, sales billing, accounts payable, and payroll. A variation analysis will be performed of all accounts with significant changes in comparison with the 19xx year-end balance. A review of the August 30, 19xx, physical inventory compilation and a follow-up of previous audit comments will also be conducted.

Background

Sam Pole's Best Ozone Paint—located in Anytown, USA—is a key location for the company's ozone paint manufacturing. It joined the companies in 19xx and experienced several start-up problems.

Figure 3.4 Continued

Financial Highlights
for the six months ended June 30
($000's omitted)

Balance Sheet	19xx	19xx
Inventories	$4,000	$5,000
Other Current Asset	100	300
Total Current Assets	4,100	5,300
Net Fixed Assets	13,000	15,000
Total Assets	$17,100	$20,300
Total Liabilities	12,000	14,000
Equity	5,100	6,300
Net liabilities and equity	$17,000	$20,300

Income Statement	19xx	19xx
Net Sales	$24,000	$35,000
Cost of Sales	18,800	23,500
Gross Profit	5,200	11,500
SG&A	3,200	7,500
Net Income before Taxes	$ 2,000	$ 4,000

Significant Audit Areas/Audit Approach

Inventory—Inventory is considered to be the most significant area at Sam Pole's Best Ozone paint manufacturing facility. Our audit procedures will include observation of the physical inventory, testing of the system of internal controls, testing of the inventory compilation, review, and testing of the roll forward from the physical to September 30, 19xx.

Payables—Payables are significant because of the amount of volume and its interrelationship with inventory. Our procedures will include flowcharting and testing of the system, testing of cutoff, vouching of selected account, reviewing and preparing reconciliations of vendor statements and examining subsequent payments.

Figure 3.4 Continued

Other Balance Sheet Accounts—Our approach to auditing these accounts will be to perform an analytical review to compare current year balances to prior year and accounting for all significant changes. Substantive audit procedures will be used on all material balances.

Other Areas

Other areas which will be given emphasis in the current audit include:

- Analysis of repair and maintenance accounts
- Analysis of all outside service accounts
- Review of controls over customer returns.

Staff and Timing

The audit will be conducted by both the Internal Audit Manager and J. Smith, a new audit senior. Field-work will begin on October 26 and will last for two weeks.

Budget (in man hours)

Planning	6
Supervision	2
General	4
Meetings, tours, etc.	4
Analytical review	4
Flowcharting and	
review of systems controls:	
Inventory ledger	12
Purchasing/Accounts Payable	8
Payroll	8
Sales/Billing	8
Cycle Tests	10
Trial Balance	3
Cash	2
Accounts Receivable	4
Inventory	20
Fixed Assets	6
Other Assets	3
Accounts Payable	6

SAM POLE COMPANY

(LOGO)

CORPORATE AUDIT DEPARTMENT

PROCEDURES MANUAL

DATE:

TITLE: Performance Process Matrix

NO: 3.1

PAGES:

Figure 3.4 Continued

Accruals 4
Income and Expense 6
Internal Control
      Questionnaire Review 4
Travel 4
Finalization of W/P 8
Report 16
              TOTAL: **152**

This will assist all parties in understanding the areas of concern and how these areas are to be audited.

Staff and Timing—This section lists the staff assigned to the audit, their job level, and the dates assigned to the audit. Planning in this area is necessary to ensure that the field work will be completed within the audit budget.

Budget—The audit budget is a compromise between what we would like to do and what we can effectively allow time for in meeting our overall departmental objectives. Normally, the total hours will be estimated in a three-year plan. An appraisal is made of the objective and scope of work to be performed and the number of hours to complete each area of the assignments. The hours for each area should agree with total budgeted hours.

(e)   Audit Status Report

The purpose of a status report is to provide audit management with a progress report of the assignment. On assignments scheduled for more than four weeks, a status report is required. A typical report would outline significant findings, audit scope changes and reasons, work completed and an estimate of time to complete the assignment. This information enables the manager to make a decision on additional scope changes, staffing (increase/decrease) and staff schedule changes.

The in-charge auditor has the responsibility for the status report. In some instances, due to the importance of the matter, the manager will issue a memo to the Director of Auditing.

A formal status report is not usually required for short period assignments. However, an informal report can be phoned into the manager describing significant findings, the status of work completed, the estimate of time of completion, and other situations affecting the audit.

Communication with the manager keeps him aware of current situations and assists in the decision making on that assignment as well as scheduling other audits. It also provides documentation, as required in our corporate audit performance process, in our project control file.

(f) Developing Audit Recommendations

An audit recommendation is a condition which, in the auditor's judgment, requires change or action and which is of sufficient magnitude to warrant the attention of management. Discovery of an exception is the starting point in development of a recommendation. When an exception is revealed during audit testing, development of a recommendation may require a series of expanded audit tests, research, and communication. The problem or situation as it exists must be fully defined and explained. The ability to express the results of an audit in well-written audit recommendations is a measure of assurance that management will take appropriate action and one of the principal bases on which audit performance will be judged. Each auditor must assume individual responsibility for improving his proficiency in this respect.

A. Basic Criteria

Some basic criteria for effective writing which should be observed in the preparation of audit recommendations are as follows:

1. *Accuracy*—Recommendations in audit reports must be verified thoroughly so that there are no factual errors. The auditor should be careful not to use data which could be misleading.

2. *Objectivity*—Include all significant, relevant information, even if it indicates disagreement with the auditor's position. Do not rely on inferences and implications. Adequate background information should be provided so that the reader can grasp the significance of the situation reported.

3. *Readability*—In preparing an audit recommendation, the auditor should be continuously conscious of how it will be perceived by the reader. Avoid disagreeable or inflammatory tone, sarcasm, ridicule, or oratory. Try to foresee the reader's reactions to certain words or phrases and be tactful. The use of correct grammar and proper punctuation is an imperative for well-written audit recommendations.

4. *Clarity*—To the extent possible, clarity should be interpreted as requiring that every statement cannot only be understood, but that it cannot reasonably be misunderstood.

B. General Characteristics

1. Evaluate the significance of what you are reporting.

2. Write in simple, nontechnical, and clear language.

3. If you refer to a form number, state its name or subject somewhere in the report.

4. If you use abbreviations, spell out their meaning when they first appear.

5. Reasonableness of logic is important.

6. Be concise. Avoid wordiness and inclusion of extraneous matter.

7. Do not be evasive. If you have something to say and can support it, then say it.

8. Write constructively. Stress the need for improvements in the future rather than focusing on deficiencies in the past.

9. All information in recommendations must be adequately supported.

10. Present relevant comments and reviews of the issues being discussed.

11. Opinions should be clearly identified as such, especially if they concern significant matters.

12. Do not generalize by simply saying that a practice "weakens controls." You should be able to say how it weakens controls.

C. Development Process

The following steps should be followed in order to provide for systematic development of a recommendation after an exception is revealed:

1. The problem or situation as it exists must be fully defined and explained.

2. The criteria or standards for an activity should be re-evaluated as to applicability and adequacy at this point in the development of the recommendation. Some criteria as to the performance of the activity must be established based on authority, generally accepted principles, or reasonableness.

3. It is necessary to look at the effect and significance of the problem. Through further testing and gathering of data, the extent of a problem and its importance must be determined. Efforts should be made to obtain quantification in the gathering of measures of effect.

4. If the effect is minimal, this is the auditor's notice to discuss the problem with the operating level of management. A recommendation is not required in an audit report when the effect is minimal.

5. If, in the auditor's opinion, the effect is significant, the auditor should proceed with the development of the recommendation.

6. The auditor must seek to find out, through expanded testing and gathering of data, what caused the problem or situation. Frequently, this is the most difficult step in the

SAM POLE COMPANY

(LOGO)

CORPORATE AUDIT DEPARTMENT

.PROCEDURES MANUAL

DATE:

TITLE: Performance Process Matrix

NO: 3.1

PAGES:

development of an audit recommendation. However, without it, you have an incomplete recommendation and can offer management only a correction of the existing problem. You cannot provide a statement of action that will give assurance that a situation will not recur.

If the actual cause of a problem cannot be disclosed through expanded testing and gathering of data, the auditor should discuss the situation with responsible management. Obtain response as to what would improve the condition or situation. Based on the outcome of this discussion with the auditee, the auditor will be guided as to the statement of action that should be made for correcting the condition. If an actual cause of the condition is revealed, the statement of action should be directed at the correction of the cause. A discussion with the responsible management as to the problem, the criteria, the effect, and the cause should be held to obtain their comments in order to further substantiate the accuracy of the developed recommendation.

D. Developing Recommendation Data

1. *Statement of Condition*—In this section, the auditor should state the circumstances surrounding the recommendation. In a logical sequence, present the facts and specific illustrations describing the condition. Each statement of condition must contain sufficient qualitative and quantitative information to fully support the conclusions or main point. The statement of condition should be brief, but not to the point where completeness is sacrificed.

2. *Criteria*—The criteria represent the standards against which the auditor is measuring a questionable condition or practice. The criteria applied may vary; however, the auditor should concentrate on the criteria which are important to the objective of the audit. Some examples of criteria are:

   a. Written requirements (laws, regulations, instructions, manuals, directives, etc)

   b. Independent opinion of experts outside the organization

   c. Prudent business practice

   d. Verbal instruction

   e. Managerial expertise

   f. Unwritten overall objectives as explained by management officials

   g. Common sense.

   Published criteria may be directly quoted, summarized, or paraphrased. If criteria are not already set forth in writing, the auditor may have to obtain information which will serve as evidence of criteria. If commonsense subjective judgment is to be used as a criterion, it should be both logical and convincing to the reader.

3. *Effect*—Effect is the actual or potential adverse impact, which has resulted or can result from the condition being questioned, in dollars or other terms. Some examples of effect are:

   a. Uneconomical or inefficient use of resources (time, money, manpower)

   b. Loss of potential income

   c. Violation of law

   d. Funds improperly spent

   e. Information or records which are meaningless or inaccurate

   f. Ineffectiveness; the job not being accomplished as well as it could be or as intended

   g. Inadequate control or loss of control over resources or actions

   h. Lack of assurance that the job is being done properly

   i. Lack of assurance that objectives are being met. If the auditor does not present information on the actual or potential adverse effect, the reader might assume that the apparent lack of concern means that the recommendation is not very important. If the effect is not significant, the recommendation should not be included in the report. Caution should be exercised not to create an issue larger than facts actually warrant.

4. *Cause*—The cause is the underlying reason why questionable behavior or condition occurred. This sensitive and usually highly judgmental area requires the most penetrating efforts and insights of the auditor. As a minimum effort, the auditor should have explored the situation deeply enough so that he can generate what is termed a "first level statement of action." That is, one that is sufficiently detailed or specific enough to enable the recipient of the recommendation to correct the conditions. It is necessary to get as close to the real cause of the problem as possible, or least to one or more causes which will put the recommendation in perspective, make the recommendation convincing and lead to a sensitive, specific statement of corrective action. Simply stating that the problem or adverse condition exists because someone did not comply with company policy is not very meaningful. Also, this approach usually confines the auditor to the rather superficial statement of action that they "comply with company policy." The following are some examples of cause:

   a. Lack of training

   b. Lack of communications

   c. Unfamiliarity with requirements

   d. Negligence or carelessness

   e. Guidelines or standards (criteria) are inadequate, not provided, obsolete, or impractical

   f. Conscious decision or instruction to deviate from requirements (for any of a variety of reasons)

   g. Lack of resources (funds or staff)

   h. Failure to use good judgment or common sense

   i. Dishonesty

   j. Lack of effective or sufficient supervision, or lack of supervisory review

   k. Unwillingness to change

   l. Lack of planning, faulty or ineffective organizational arrangement, or delegations of authority.

5. *Statement of Action*—Generally, each recommendation will result in one or more statements of action. Experience indicates a great receptivity to constructive audit statements of action. The following are some basic guidelines for developing statements of action.

   a. Present statements of action as a logical sequence to the related statement of conditions.

   b. Present statements of action that are as specific, realistic, and as helpful as possible and related directly to the cause of the weakness or deficiency. State what action will provide a meaningful solution to the problems, and not simply recommend that "regulations be complied with;" "controls be strengthened;" or "procedures be established."

   c. Direct the statements of action toward the audited organization and to the specific persons, by title, who have responsibility and authority to take corrective action.

   d. Do not include statements of action on which adequate action has been taken before the report is issued. Instead, report, in the body of the recommendation, what action has been taken to correct the situation and only present additional statements of recommended action as warranted.

e. Avoid the use of extreme language in making statements of action, such as "immediately," "expedite," "without delay," "as soon as possible," unless the nature of the problem is so serious that such language seems particularly appropriate.

f. The expression "for consideration" should not be used in presenting statements of action. Since the Audit Department is a staff function and its service advisory, all statements of action are for "consideration."

g. Material, thoughts, or information that were not developed in the body of the recommendation should not be introduced in the statement of action. The statement of action should follow logically from what is presented in the recommendation.

(i) Recommendation Worksheet

A form should be created for the purpose of writing up the recommendations as they are initially discovered (see Figure 3.5 for an example of a worksheet format). A copy should then be given to the auditee. There are many good reasons for following this procedure.

1. If recommendations are neat and well written at the time of discovery and copies given to the auditee, valuable research and input can be obtained before the closing conference. This makes the closing conference more productive as both sides are knowledgeable on the subject. Generally, the auditee is blindsided at the closing conference if recommendations have not been previously presented.

2. The procedure lends itself to better written, more factual audit recommendations because the material is fresh on the auditor's mind as opposed to trying to write the recommendation later in time. Strengths and weaknesses can be reconciled to improve the quality of the recommendations.

3. Why take many recommendations to the closing conference when a "climate for change" can be initiated during the course of the audit. Too many recommendations presented at one time tends to make the auditee nervous and worry about how the report is going to look to others. Tentative recommendations should be provided to the auditee periodically, once a week, and not on a daily basis.

4. If the recommendation has been resolved by the auditee during the audit, it is much more agreeable to the auditee if only mention is made summarizing items corrected during the audit.

5. The interim communication also gives the auditor a written workpaper document to use in discussing recommendations at the closing conference.

6. Once written recommendations are resolved to the degree possible, needed corrections should be made and submitted for typing of the final report.

Figure 3.5 Recommendation Worksheet Example

Audit Job No. _____
Recommendation No. _____
Workpaper Ref. _____

Auditee _____   _____ Audit Date

STATEMENT OF CONDITION: (What is) _____

CRITERIA: (What it should be) _____

EFFECT: (So what) _____

CAUSE: (Reason for deviation) _____

STATEMENT OF ACTION: _____

PRESENT STATUS: _____
    Recommendation corrected during audit _____
    Auditee agreed with recommendation _____
    Detailed support for adjustment/correction provided to auditee _____
    In process of implementing _____
    Auditee disagrees with recommendation/comment _____

Preparer signature: _____

Senior Auditor signature: _____

Provide a copy of this completed form to auditee ASAP/Use form for the Closing Conference.

(ii)   Form Format

The form is designed to be as functional as possible, but it is limited in space to encourage factual, precise write-up of recommendations.

Recommendation/Discussion Item—A recommendation is a material exception to corporate policy, procedures, as examples, which are controllable by the auditee. The auditee is required to submit a written response to the recommendations. A discussion item is also an exception which may be material, but is not controlled by the auditee. Therefore, the auditee is not required to respond to the discussion item.

Audit—Write the name of the branch or location in the space provided to facilitate audit identification.

Subject—Identify the subject area where the exception occurred as payroll, accounts payable, for example:

> CAJ No.—Corporate Audit Job Number
> CAR No.—Corporate Audit Recommendation Number

Corporate Audit Job Numbers will be standardized and assigned by the audit division offices.

Corporate Audit Recommendation Number is the sequenced number of the recommendation developed as the audit work progresses. The Corporate Audit Recommendation Number is to be used as a control point.

Recommendation/Facts—Remembering that a statement of action is a call for action by management and must be written on that basis, the facts follow the attributes of a recommendation:

> A. Statement of condition (What is)
> B. Criteria (What it should be)
> C. Effect (So what)
> D. Cause (Reason for deviation).

Present Status—A space provided for comments offered by the auditee which will give light to their intentions or reaction to the audit recommendation. It may only be necessary to check one of the preprinted comments such as "Recommendation Implemented During Audit."

SAM POLE COMPANY	LOGO	CORPORATE AUDIT DEPARTMENT	
		PROCEDURES MANUAL	DATE:
TITLE: Workpapers		NO: 3.2	PAGES:

3.2 WORKPAPERS

Workpapers serve mainly to: (1) aid the auditor in the conduct of his work and (b) provide important support for the auditor's opinion. Such language as "Workpapers are a record . . . of tests and procedures." "Workpapers, accordingly, may include work programs, analysis memoranda, letters of representation, confirmations, abstracts of company documents and schedules and commentaries prepared by the auditor," further attempt to describe workpapers and some of their contents. Other comments such as "Workpapers should fit the circumstances and the auditor's needs on the engagement to which they apply," are from SAS No. 1, Section 338. Although SASs are written for the public accountant, these comments are applicable to the corporate auditor because the same quality is required for the external auditors to place any reliance on our workpapers. It is imperative to establish standards of compliance to help ensure quality workpapers.

Before preparation, consideration should be given to what the objectives are for creating your workpapers. Only information supporting your objectives is to be included. Envision how the workpaper will look after it is completed. Does it appear *logically organized*, relevant, and neat without half erasures, figures and comments that do not appear crowded together and is it *complete* without loose ends to be accounted for?

A second thought, and one that should be seriously considered, is that the IRS can and has subpoenaed internal auditors' workpapers into court. The question is, would you be embarrassed if your workpaper was made a document of the court? What if the court made an enlargement of your workpaper and it was displayed on a screen for all to see?

Other factors to consider in developing workpapers are:

Control

Retention

Headings

Permanent Files—Contents and Format

Current Files—Contents and Format

General Organization

Detailed Workpaper Section Organization

Indexing and Cross Referencing

Referencing

Standard Tick Marks

(a) Control

For Corporate Audit purposes, workpapers are confidential documents used to support our conclusions. In order to maintain our independence and protect confidentiality, audit bags containing workpapers must be locked if left overnight at the auditee's office.

During working hours, workpapers should be retained in a controlled, orderly fashion. That is, they should not be left lying around the work area or left out in the auditee's office where they can be seen, handled, or misplaced by the auditee employees.

In the office, workpapers should be filed in secured cabinets. During work hours, care should be exercised ensuring that visitors do not inadvertently observe confidential information lying on desks. Prior to leaving the office, workpapers should be secured in locked cabinets or desks.

(b) Retention

The retention period for both workpapers and reports is five years. If an exception arises where the retention period is to be extended beyond this period, a notation should be boldly printed on the outside cover of the workpaper binder or on the face of the report which would indicate the destruction date.

(c) Headings

In order to standardize Corporate Audit workpaper headings, the following information should be used for all workpapers:

Description on Workpapers	Location on Workpapers
Name of auditee-location	Top-Center
As-of date of audit	Top-Center
Identification of workpaper	Top-Center
Initials of auditor performing work	Bottom-Right (area provided)
Initials of in-charge senior manager	Bottom-Right
Workpaper index (red pencil only)	Bottom-Right (area provided)

WORKPAPER "DOS" AND "DON'TS"

Do

1. While the audit is in progress, prepare a to-do list of points that have not been resolved.

2. Resolve points with auditee at one time during the day.

3. Be neat, write legibly, use a medium-hard lead pencil, keep figures in proper columns.

4. Use a ruler; single line for subtotals, double lines for totals.

5. Avoid crowding on a single page.

6. Be accurate; be sure amounts are accurate and footings are correct.

7. Head every workpaper (see headings).

8. Identify the source of information on each workpaper, reference books or original entry, voucher numbers, conversations with employees, and so on. Distinguish between fact and opinion.

9. If a workpaper is prepared by auditee, indicate with "PBA" on workpaper. Indicate the name of employee performing task.

10. Initial and date each workpaper.

11. Indicate analysis which requires more than one workpaper by: 1 of 5, 2 of 5, and so on.

12. Adequately explain all tick marks other than the standard tick marks. Summarize explanations at the bottom of each workpaper by using a legend.

13. Use proper grammar.

14. When referring to auditee employees, spell their names and their titles completely and correctly.

15. Indicate clearly the extent of tests made.

16. Write your opinions and conclusions using care to differentiate among facts, opinions, and explanation.

17. All memoranda should be prepared on memo pad paper. Skip every other line and write only to the right-hand margin line.

18. Write on just one side of a working paper.

19. Remove all items that have no value in supporting the conclusion.

20. Verify that the final figures on each workpaper agree with the lead sheets, working trial balance, and cross-reference thereto.

21. Reference and cross-reference to other workpaper and interim recommendation worksheets.

22. Leave enough space on each working paper to clearly identify adjusting entries and comments.

23. Use legal size paper only.

24. Use red pencil.

Don't

1. Don't prepare workpapers without first considering the objectives.

2. Don't follow previous audit workpapers blindly, but have a logical reason for changes.

3. Don't prepare separate income and expense account analyses when the accounts can be more effectively covered in conjunction with balance sheet items.

4. Don't leave open points or questions on your workpapers.

5. Don't merely cross over points or questions, but explain disposition.

6. Don't repeat scope of work when steps are outlined in audit program. Indicate audit program followed.

7. Don't make workpapers available to anyone without prior approval from the manager.

(d)   Permanent Files—Contents and Format

Permanent files are to be used for documents which will be needed in audits for a number of years. The binder should be labeled "Permanent Folder" and contain an index showing the contents of the folder.

Permanent files should be economical in content. They should not be cluttered with documents that can't effectively help or provide information for future audits.

Figure 3.6 outlines the format of the permanent file. This will also act as the index for the file.

For example, consider A-Corporate Audit Reports/Responses. The first report entered into the permanent folder will be indexed in A-1, the second in A-2, and so on.

Each document entered into the permanent file must include the date and initials of the auditor. Revisions or modifications must also be initialized and dated. Use red pencil for this purpose.

(e)   Current Files—Contents and Format

The criterion for determining whether information should be included either in the permanent file or the current file is the useful life of the information. Place information into the permanent file if the usefulness of the information is longer than two years. The majority of information obtained during an audit usually applies to the current year and will only be used for comparison and guidance in the

Figure 3.6   Permanent Files Index

Sam Pole Company
Corporate Audit Department
Permanent Folder Index

A. Corporate Audit Reports/Responses

B. Reports—Other

C. Carry Forward Comments

D. Organization Charts/Key Personnel

E. Internal Control Questionnaires/ Audit Programs

F. Contracts/Lease Agreements

G. Labor Agreements

H. Historical Information/Pictures/Nature of Business Unit

I. Correspondence (Major)

J. Excerpts from Meeting (i.e., plant, branch, board)

K. Company Directives Memorandums

L. Account Analysis

M. Other

subsequent year. Accordingly, such expected useful life would be less than two years and is filed in the current file.

(f) General Organization

Use the printed workpaper binder cover and back furnished by the department. Note that certain information is to be completed on the cover of the binder: company identification, contents of the binder, the names of auditors who worked on sections included in the binder, review signatures, and the name of the audit office producing the file.

Acco fasteners have 2-3/4-inch centers with 2-inch capacity. If files exceed 2 inches, Acco fasteners of greater capacity can be obtained.

All workpapers are to be 8-1/2 inch by 14 inches, legal size. If auditee documents are less than legal size, attach the document to heavy-grade legal size paper. Do not waste memo or seven-column paper for this purpose.

Create dividers by using heavy-grade paper and attaching a tab at the bottom of the sheet. A second method is to use 14-column paper as a wraparound for the individual section. The section name and indexing letter should be indicated in red at the bottom right hand corner after the 14-column paper is folded in half.

(g) Detailed Workpaper Section Organization

Each job will have a systems binder to be updated yearly. The following sequence will be utilized to organize the systems binder where the "S" denotes systems documentation work.

SA-1	Flowchart (manual/EDP)
SA-2	Narrative description
SA-3	List of key reports (official report title and informal user name)
SA-4	Internal control questionnaire
SA-5	Summary of major strengths and weaknesses
SA-6	Audit approach memo
SA-7	Other systems information as needed

The compliance and substantive work for each account will be organized in the following sequence in a separate current file:

A/C	Overall scope and conclusion
A/P	Audit program
A	Lead sheets

A-1 to A-xx   Account detail (substantive testing), cycle testing (compliance testing), comments for future audits and confirmation forms; detailed audit work supporting lead sheet balances.

NOTE: The audit procedures performed and workpapers generated should be organized in a manner deemed to be logical and expedient in the senior's judgment.

SA-1, Flowcharting—Include both the manual and data-processing flow of documents as you flowchart the system. Graphically depict the inputs, processing, and outputs of each system.

SA-2, Narrative System Description—Narratives may be used to describe a system on a step-by-step basis. The narrative system description can supplement flowcharts or stand alone if it best fits the system.

SA-3, Key reports listing—The key report listing should list important reports by their official title and also by informal names used by the auditee. This listing will greatly assist the following year's audit.

SA-4, Internal control evaluation guide—The internal control evaluation guide should be developed to include only questions applicable to the section involved. "A" the cash section, should include the internal control questionnaire evaluation guides only for cash.

SA-5, Summary of major strengths and weaknesses—Once the flowchart and internal control questionnaire have been prepared, a summary of the system's major strengths and weaknesses should be prepared. This will aid in the development of the audit approach.

SA-6, Audit approach memo—Based on the above procedures, the auditor should have a good idea for the strengths and weaknesses of the system. The logic behind the selected audit procedures should be written up in a memorandum and included in this section.

A/C, Overall scope and conclusion—This workpaper will be the last item completed in the section, but it is first in the organization sequence. Identify the work involved to support your conclusion; procedures such as sample size, extent of testing, and compliance to audit program. In the conclusion section, state your opinion based upon the testing performed in the scope. Make references and cross-references to adjustments and recommendations or comments that are the result of your work.

A/P, Audit programs—Audit programs should include all the steps necessary to test the system and reach a logical conclusion. Such tests will include substantive tests of account balances and compliance tests of the system.

A, Lead sheets—The auditor should give advance thought to the preparation of lead sheets. Minimum information includes a comparative schedule showing account balances at the prior year audit date and the book balance for the current audit date. Also, columns are prepared for adjustments and final balances. These schedules should reference to the working trial balance.

A-1–A-XX, Account detail (substantive testing)—The evidential matter obtained through two general classes of auditing procedures: (a) test of details of transactions and balances and (b) analytical reviews of significant ratios and trends and the investigation of unusual fluctuations and questionable items.

A-100–A-XXX, Cycle testing (compliance testing)—The purpose for tests of compliance is to provide reasonable assurance that accounting control procedures are being applied as prescribed.

(h) Indexing and Cross Referencing

Workpapers should be indexed using the prescribed standard index. Each schedule should be marked in red pencil in the designated box at the bottom right corner. The index is then utilized throughout the files whenever a cross-indexing reference is made to that particular schedule or to an amount therein.

An index has been assigned to each major account classification. Single alpha letters are used for asset section designations. Double alpha letters are used for liabilities on capital accounts. Numbers are used to indicate accounts in the income statement. These sections will be preceded by "PL," before the number indicated later in the index sample.

The first section of the indexing system is referred to as the administrative section. The index to reference this section is "AD."

The workpaper sections will include subaccounts under the major account classification. For example, cash, the major account, also includes subaccounts of cash in bank, cash on hand, etc. The lead sheet (indexed "A") for this section should show the applicable subaccount balances for the current period and the prior period. These columns should be footed to show the total balance in the major account. The analysis of the subaccounts should be documented on supporting schedules (i.e., A-1—analysis of cash in bank, A-2—analysis of cash on hand, etc.)

Occasionally, a section within a file binder may become too large to control effectively. In that instance, the section may be extended into another binder. The indexing for the extended file binder becomes X. For example, if section CC accounts payable becomes too large, part of the file can be stored in another file binder indexed CCX. Appropriate referencing should be indicated in the working papers.

Three separate sections have been included for the work performed on Confirmations, Inventory Observation, and Inventory Compilation. The section for Confirmations is to be used when the number of confirmations sent is too large to be practically included in the applicable account classification. The other two sections are to be used when a physical inventory observation and a review of the inventory compilation are included within the scope of the audit. Be sure to appropriately reference these sections in the working papers.

The following is a listing of the indexes which should be used:

Administrative

AD1   Copy of audit report
AD2   Assignment checklist
AD3   Copy of financial statements
AD4   Summary memo—in-charge
AD5   Manager comments—interpretive comments, major problems and their solutions
AD6   Working trial balances
AD7   Adjusting journal entries
AD8   Analytical review and interim financial statements
AD9   Audit planning memo
AD10 Time budget
AD11 Interim audit recommendations and comments summary
      (AUD from 1)
AD12 Prior audit reports and follow-up
AD13 Other correspondence
AD14 As needed

Index   *Description*

                    Assets

A   Cash
B   Securities and other negotiable assets
C   Sales, shipping, and trade receivables
D   Intercompany receivables
E
F   Inventory
G   Prepaid expenses and other assets
H
I
J
K
M   Other intangible assets
S   Property plant and equipment

Liabilities

BB	Notes payable
CC	Accounts payable
DD	Accounts payable intercompany
FF	Compensation
GG	
HH	Other liabilities and deferred credits
WW	Capital stock and surplus
PP	Notes and intercompany debt

Income Statement and Other

PL1	Sales and revenue
PL2	Cost at goods sold
PL3	Selling, general and administrative expenses
X	Extended file

(i) Referencing

Normally, detail subschedules support the amounts shown on the lead schedules. Also, the lead schedules support the amounts shown on the trial balance. These workpapers should be cross-referenced to one another. Referencing should be done by inserting the page index next to the corresponding amount. Writing the page index to the right of the amount indicates "going to" a certain page. Writing the page index to the left of the amount indicates "coming from" a certain page. The referencing of final totals (double underscored) may be done by inserting the page index directly below the applicable amount.

When referencing on the same page, either a circled number or a circled capital letter should be used. A circled number is used when referencing a number to a number. A circled capital letter is used when referencing a number (or any other section or symbol on the working paper) to a note. All referencing should be done in red pencil.

(j) Standard Tick Marks

Standardizing certain tick marks will result in uniformity and time-saving for the preparer and reviewer by duplicating the tick marks and writing one explanation. Tick marks should be simple in design. Always explain tick marks in a legend located in the workpapers. Use a "Standard Tick Mark Sheet" to explain standard tick marks. Basic tick marks should be placed after the figure being checked. Prepare all tick marks in red pencil.

Standard tick marks are as follows:

F (under number)	footed
F (to right of number)	cross-footed
T/B	agreed to trial balance
G/L	agreed to general ledger

3.3 AUDIT OBJECTIVES

As described in Chapter 2 of this Manual, the Corporate Audit Department may be responsible for conducting a variety of different types of audits. These types of audits may have different overall objectives that the auditor must satisfy through the performance of audit procedures.

The most common type of audit that we are responsible for is the financial audit. Broadly described, the overall objective of a financial audit is to assure that the financial statements are fairly stated, that they are in conformity with GAAP and that the accounting principles that were applied are consistent from year to year. In order to satisfy this overall objective, it is necessary to satisfy specific objectives that apply to the various accounts that comprise the financial statements. The following is a listing of objectives that apply to the various audit areas (accounts) that are normally included in a financial audit. This listing is not all-inclusive and all of the objectives may not apply in every circumstance. They should be used as a guide and should be included, excluded, and/or modified as dictated by the audit situations encountered.

Cash

- Cash recorded properly represent cash and cash items on hand, in transit, or in banks

- Adequate disclosure is made of restricted or committed funds and of cash not subject to immediate withdrawal

- All receipts are properly identified, deposited, and recorded

- All intercompany and interbank transfers are properly accounted for

- All bank accounts and cash on hand are subject to effective custodial accountability procedures and physical safeguards.

Receivables

- Recorded receivables exist and are carried at net collectible amounts

- All collections are properly identified, control totals are developed, and collections promptly deposited

- Billings and collections are properly recorded in individual customer accounts

- Allowance for doubtful accounts is adequate.

Inventories

- Physical inventories are taken and are valued in accordance with company policies which are in accordance with GAAP

- The quantities properly represent products, materials, and supplies on hand, in transit, in storage, or on consignment that belong to the company

- All receipts, transfers, and withdrawals of stock are properly and accurately recorded

- All production activity and costs are properly and accurately reported and maintained in up-to-date cost records

- The items are priced in accordance with GAAP, consistently applied, at the lower of cost or market

- Excess, slow-moving, obsolete, and defective items are reduced to net realizable values

- Adequate provision for losses on purchases or sales commitments exist

- The ending inventories are determined as to quantities, prices, computations, excess stocks, etc., on a basis consistent with the inventories at the end of the preceding year.

Investments

- The physical evidences of the ownership of investments are on hand or held in custody or safekeeping by others for account of the company

- The basis on which the investments are stated is in accordance with GAAP, consistently applied

- All purchases or sales are initiated by authorized individuals and are properly approved

- Income from investments has been accounted for properly.

Fixed Assets

- All recorded assets exist

- The basis upon which the property accounts are stated is proper, conforms with GAAP, and has been consistently followed

- All productive asset transactions are initiated by authorized individuals after advance approval has been obtained

- The additions during the period under audit are proper capital charges and represent actual physical property installed or constructed

- Adequate cost records are maintained for all in-progress and completed projects

- Physical inventories of recorded productive assets are taken at periodic intervals

- Depreciation charged to income during the period is adequate but not excessive and has been computed on an acceptable basis consistent with that used in prior periods

- The balance in depreciation reserve accounts are reasonable, considering the expected useful lives of the property units and possible net salvage values.

Other Assets

- Recorded prepaid and deferred expenses represent proper charges against future operations

- The additions during the audit period are proper charges to those accounts and represent actual cost

- Amortization or write-offs against revenues in the current period and to date are reasonable under the circumstances and have been computed on an acceptable basis consistent with prior periods.

Purchasing, Accounts Payable, Disbursements

- All costs are properly recorded and classified as expense, inventory, fixed assets, and other assets

- All purchase requisitions are initiated and approved by authorized individuals

- All material and services received agree with original purchase orders

- All invoices processed for payment represent goods and services received and are accurate as to terms, quantities, prices, extensions, and account distributions

- All checks are prepared on the basis of adequate and approved documentation and are compared with supporting data

- All checks are properly approved, signed, and mailed

- All disbursements are properly recorded

- All accrued expenses relate to goods and services received as of the end of the fiscal period.

Notes and Loans Payable

- All amounts owed are properly recorded

- Accrued interest has been recorded

- Compliance with all provisions of loan agreements has occurred

- All debt transactions are initiated by authorized individuals and are approved by the Board of Directors or executives to whom this authority has been delegated.

Capital Stock and Surplus

- The capital stock and surplus accounts are properly classified, described, and stated in accordance with GAAP, and are not in conflict with the requirements of the corporate charter (or articles of incorporation) or with the applicable statutes of the state of incorporation

- Transactions in the capital stock and surplus accounts during the audit period are properly authorized or approved where necessary and are recorded in accordance with GAAP.

Revenues, Costs and Expenses

- Reported revenues, costs, and expenses are properly applicable to the accounting period under examination

- Reported revenues and applicable costs are recorded on a timely basis

- Charges to customers are for valid claims for sales rendered in accordance with established pricing policies

- Costs and expenses are properly matched with revenues

- Recognition has been given to revenues, costs, and expenses (including losses) which should be so recognized

- Revenues, costs, and expenses are appropriately classified and described in the statement of income.

Payroll

- Compensation costs reflect the aggregate cost of employee services during the period and are distributed to appropriate inventory and expense accounts

- Compensation rates are in accordance with applicable union agreements and/or approved rates

- Additions, separations, wage rates, salaries, and other deductions are authorized and recorded on a timely basis

- Employee time and attendance data are properly reviewed, approved, and processed on a timely basis

- Payroll deductions are determined in accordance with legal requirements or employee authorizations and are paid to the government, unions, and other specified parties

- Payment for compensation and benefits are made only to bonafide employees

- All authorized employee benefit plans and related costs are appropriately controlled and administered.

Travel & Entertainment Expense

- All expenses recorded must be "ordinary," meaning customary and usual within the experience of the particular community

- All expenses recorded must be "necessary." meaning appropriate and helpful for the development of the entity's business

- Sufficient documentation must exist. Specifically the amount, time, place, business purpose, and business relationship of the entertained party

- Reimbursements to employees must be fully accountable, so as not to be considered compensatory. If any reimbursements are compensatory, appropriate tax information must be retained.

Chapter 4

AUDIT REPORTING

SAM POLE		CORPORATE AUDIT DEPARTMENT	
COMPANY	(LOGO)	PROCEDURES MANUAL	DATE:
TITLE: Corporate Audit Report Process		NO: 4.1	PAGES:

4.1 CORPORATE AUDIT REPORT PROCESS

The Corporate Audit Report is perhaps the most significant product of the audit function. The procedures contained in this section of the Manual are designed to help ensure that the best possible quality product is prepared.

The objectives of the report process include:

- To ensure the development of comprehensive and accurate reports

- To provide guidelines resulting in timely issuance of final reports

- To provide the opportunity to convey additional related information to readers of the report.

Since the audit report is the most significant product issued by the Audit Department, the report format should be carefully considered. It is the policy of Sam Pole Company to issue a summary-and-detail report for each significant audit completed. The purpose of the summary report is to provide, in brief presentation format, the essence of the scope and results of the audit. It also allows for a profile section to convey additional information of interest to the Audit Committee and senior management. The thoughtful and creative use of the profile section provides a vehicle for the Audit Department to convey information beyond the negative reporting process that is inherent in internal auditing. To put it another way: the use of the profile section enables us to convey information that may contribute positively to the management of the corporation. In some instances, this would be basic financial or operational information which helps put the audit results in the proper context. Detailed descriptions of the summary and detailed report formats, with examples, are contained in subsequent sections of the Manual.

The reporting process begins with the draft audit comments and follows through to the issuance of reports and the report to the audit committee (if appropriate). The corporate audit reporting process matrix, Figure 4.1, summarizes the activities contained in this process.

(a) Draft Reports

The audit report process begins with a review of the tentative audit recommmendations worksheets prepared during the audit performance process. Each individual page contains comments accumulated during the audit process. These pages will have been preliminary reviewed by the auditee during the audit process. The manager will review all comments in conjunction with his review of the workpapers, ensuring that all comments are adequately supported. Within approximately one week from the completion of the audit field work—or the closing conference of the audit team—the audit manager or his designee will draft an audit finding and recommendation for each of the tentative audit recommendation worksheets. These comments will then form the basis of the detailed audit report draft.

Figure 4.1 Corporate Audit Reporting Process Matrix

	ASSIGN NUMBER DRAFT COMMENTS	ASSIGN NUMBER REPORT DISTRIBUTION WORKSHEET	DRAFT REPORTS	DRAFT TO AUDITEE	INCLUSION OF AUDITEE COMMENTS	ISSUE FINAL REPORT TO MANAGEMENT	OPEN AUDIT RESULTS AND COMMENTS	FOLLOW-UP/ COMPLIANCE AUDIT [ONE YEAR]	AUDIT COMMITTEE STATUS REPORT
PURPOSE	Document audit findings, comments and recommendations for review, approval and resolution	Log/track report preparation and distribution	Formalize audit conclusions, findings, comments, and recommendations for review, approval and reporting	Obtain agreement on facts and circumstances, substance and materiality of issues for audited entity.	Incorporate auditee responses into draft reports	Apprise Audit Committee of audit results	Identify comments to be addressed and provide an agreed-upon plan of action	Document and review resolution of audit findings	Apprise Audit Committee of status of audit results and updates
TIMING	As disclosed or periodically during audit	Regularly from completion of field work to issued report	In office upon completion of field work	Within 2 weeks following exit conference	Within 30 days following receipt	Promptly upon reply and resolution of Director of Auditing considerations	30 days following transmittal of final report	Within 5 days following due date	30 days following transmittal of status report
PREPARED BY	staff or senior	senior	senior	senior	senior	manager	auditee	senior/manager	manager
REVIEWED BY	senior or manager	manager	manager	manager	Director of Auditing	senior/manager	mgr. after senior	manager	Director of Auditing
RESPONSIBILITY	senior or manager	senior	senior/manager	manager	manager	manager	manager	manager	manager
CONTENTS DOCUMENTATION	Per tentative recommendations worksheet	Per distribution worksheet	Develop comments into summary and detailed reports (see AU/ED)	Auditee comments and responses	Revise detailed reports for auditee responses; comment in summary report on responses	Audit report to: Audit Committee			Status report to Audit Committee
DISTRIBUTION	manager	manager	manager	Financial official at audited unit; manager	comptroller and chief accountant of audited entry	(See Distribution Section AU/ED)	IA manager	manager	Audit Committee, comptroller, chief accountant of audited entry
	audit workpapers	audit workpapers	audit workpapers	audit workpapers	audit workpapers	corporate secy; IA Manager, workpapers	workpapers; IA manager, Audit Committee files	audit workpapers	audit workpapers; IA manager, Policy Committee

4.1   Corporate Audit Report Process

The audit manager will begin the preparation of the summary audit report. Information regarding the scope and highlight sections will be based on information contained within the planning, status, and summary memos as well as the detailed finding and recommendations report. The Director of Auditing will review the draft and provide input.

(b) Draft to Auditee

Various practices regarding distribution of draft audit reports to auditees exist within the Internal Auditing profession. The trade-off issues involve the interest in accuracy and fair presentation versus the issue of timeliness. Some audit department believe that timeliness is not the most critical factor, and obtaining input from auditees and incorporating it in the audit report provides for increased accuracy and more level "playing field." Still other audit departments believe that the function of the audit is to issue its comments as soon as possible and they bypass or reduce the auditee review process. The auditee will then issue a response and discussion of implementation plans.

The policy of Sam Pole Company is to review comments with the auditee as they are developed. Once the audit draft has been developed, the draft is forwarded to the auditee for review. The auditee will have two weeks to review the comments and prepare a paragraph detailing their actions or position on the comment.

Figure 4.2 provides an example of a transmittal of the report draft to audit entry and Figure 4.3 is an example of a transmittal of the report to senior financial officials.

(c) Inclusion of Auditee Comments

In our example we have decided to incorporate auditees' responses into our audit report. Upon receipt of the auditee's comments, the audit manager will review their comments and integrate them into the draft audit report. The revised draft, with the auditee comments clearly identified, is then provided to the Director of Auditing for his review. The Director of Auditing, upon satisfaction with the foregoing steps, will approve the final audit report for issuance. The audit manager will be advised of any final changes to the report and will cause his report to be dated, processed and transmitted in final form for signature and reproduction.

(i) Audit Report Responses
The objectives of monitoring audit report responses are:

- To provide a framework to monitor, obtain, and evaluate such responses from audited units

- To enable the Director of Auditing to report on the adequacy of responses to, as appropriate, senior management and the Audit Committee.

Figure 4.2   Transmittal of Report Draft to Audit Entity

Date:

To: Financial Official, Audited Entity

From: Audit Manager

Subject: Corporate Audit Report Draft

The enclosed draft of a report on the recently completed [kind of audit] at [audit location] is for limited distribution to you and the Audit Director.

Please review the draft to confirm [or not] that the recommendations and comments agree with those presented to and discussed with you at the closing audit conference. Also include your response in one or two paragraphs for inclusion in the detailed audit report. Please reply to me or (designate) by phone by (date), so that we may proceed to issue the final report.

/S/ Manager

Enclosures
cc: Audit Director

Figure 4.3   Transmittal of Report Draft to Senior Financial Officials

Date:

To: J. K. Smith

From: L. Gordon

Subject: Corporate Audit Report Draft

The enclosed draft of a report on the recently completed [kind of audit] at [audit location] has been reviewed with [financial official] at [audited entity], who is in agreement with the content of the report and detailed comments.

I would appreciate receiving your comments, if any, by [date] on the issues discussed in the report so that we may proceed to issue the final report at the next meeting of the Audit Committee.

/S/ Audit Manager

Enclosures
cc: Audit Director

Each auditor will develop and implement procedures to attain the objectives outlined above and ensure that the total audit process is completed for both this department and the public accountants.

In cases when audited units have not responded within the prescribed period of time, standard 30-day (overdue reports) and 60-day (delinquent reports) letters are to be issued by the affected auditor and Director of Auditing, respectively. (See Figures 4.4 and 4.5.)

In addition to monitoring and accounting for responses, each manager is responsible for evaluation of them to determine that satisfactory management action has or will be taken. Evaluation of responses is to be documented in the workpapers or, when pertinent, advised in writing to the public accountants.

Subsequent audit procedures to test completed/proposed corrective action would be adequately documented and outlined for either Corporate Audit or public accountants' performance. In cases where responses have not dealt satisfactorily with audit recommendations, the auditor should advise the Auditee and Audit Manager, in writing, concerning additional audit requirements and the resolution of the issues. Figure 4.7 is the standard form on which the audited unit should reply. These should be sent to the unit along with the final report.

(ii) Additional Procedures

The following amplifies the policies covering the distribution of public accountants report and related responses to ensure that they are distributed properly:

Reports of Independent (Public) Accountants

Reports on internal control recommendations are issued to the individual with overall responsibility for the location under audit (i.e., president, general manager, plant manager) and the chief financial officer. Copies are distributed to the Vice President and Comptroller, the Secretary (for the official company record) and the Audit Manager.

Management Responses

Audited entities respond in writing to internal control recommendations in accordance with the aforementioned policy. The response is addressed to the Director of Auditing with copies to the Vice President and Comptroller, other key financial officials and the Public Accountants.

The additional procedures outlined above enable implementation of effective and consistent practices to monitor and report on the results of audits by public accountants in the United States and other countries.

Figure 4.4   Overdue Response to Audit Report—30-Day Letter

Date:

To: Financial Official, Audited Unit

From: Audit Manager

Subject: Response to Audit Report

[The Corporate Audit Department]/[Public Accountants] issued its report, dated _____
on the results of its examination [covering internal accounting controls]/-
[of balance sheet _____]
for the period ended _____ [date].

This is to remind you that a written response to the audit report is due no later than thirty days following the report transmittal date. Please advise when we can expect your response.

Audit Manager

cc: Audit Director
    Public Accountants (if appropriate)

Figure 4.5   Delinquent Response to Audit Report—60-Day Letter

Date:

To: Financial Official, Audited Unit

From: Audit Manager

Subject: Response to Audit Report

Sixty days have now passed since [the Corporate Audit Department]/[Public Accountants] issued its report, dated _____, on the results of its examination [covering internal accounting controls]/ [of balance sheet accounts]/of [_____] for the _____ ended [date].

You will recall that _____, our manager in _____, reminded you one month earlier that corporate policy requires a written response to the audit report no later than thirty days following the report transmittal date.

In the event you have compelling reasons for not responding, please call me or _____ immediately. Otherwise, we expect your response within a week's time. My responsibilities to the Audit Committee and senior management require regular reports on the adequacy and timeliness of responses to audit reports.

Audit Manager

cc: Audit Director
    Public Accountants (if appropriate)

Figure 4.6   Transmittal of Policy on Reports of Public Accountants

Date:

To: Audit Manager

From: Audit Director

Subject: Reports of Independent Public Accountants

Purpose

This memorandum provides additional procedures implementing the policy covering the distribution of reports of independent accountants and, when required, management responses to them.

Policy

The Sam Pole auditing policy states the following:

> Audit findings, recommendations and other matters deemed to be significant by the public accountants are reported directly by them to the Audit Manager, Chief Financial Officer, and the Audit Committee.

The policy further requires with respect to management responses:

> A prompt formal written response to the Audit Manager, covering internal control and management recommendations made by both the public accountants and corporate auditors. Responses are due no later than thirty days following the date of the auditor's report and in the format as shown on attached Figure 4.7.

Figure 4.7   Audit Response

COMPANY _____

Operating Unit: _____

Audited by: _____

Submitted By: _____

No.	Recommendation	Implementation	Responsible Person	Target Date

(d)   Issue Final Report to Management

After approval by the Director of Auditing, the final report will be distributed in accordance with the distribution policy discussed in the following sections of the Manual. It should be noted that there will be different levels of distribution for the summary and detailed reports. However, anyone receiving the summary report can request a copy of the detailed report.

(i)   Audit Report Format

The audit report and the detailed recommendations and comments sections have a standard format which will be adequate for writing most reports. There may be times when it will be appropriate to deviate from the standard format. These instances must be discussed with the manager before proceeding. Figure 4.9 is an example of an audit report.

(ii)   Standard Format

I. Audit Report—Summary	II. In-depth Recommendations and Comments—Detail
Heading	Cover Page (Optional)
Salutations	Heading
Lead Paragraph	Lead Paragraph
Profile	Categories
Scope	Recommendations
Conclusion	Comments
Summary	Discussion Items
Manager's Signature	Manager's Signature
Distribution	Exhibits (Optional)

I. Audit Report—Summary

Heading—The heading is preprinted on the Corporate Audit Report preprinted form. Company/ location, Audit Date, Audit Office, and Audit Manager are all self-explanatory.

Date Audit Completed—The date of the closing conference or last day of field work, whichever is later.

Auditors—All auditors who participated in the audit. Use the first two initials in all names.

Date of Report—The date the report is issued for distribution.

Salutation—This will generally be addressed as follows:

The Audit Committee
Sam Pole Company

Lead paragraph—The lead or introduction paragraph indicates to the Audit Committee that this report is a summary of the results of our audit or review. It makes reference to the detail section that recommendations and comments have with local management and require a response. It also states that the detail has been distributed to key officials and the Public Accountants.

It should not be necessary to restate the auditee's name or dates, since this information is included in the heading. Figure 4.8 provides an example of a lead paragraph.

Profile—"Profile" is generally preceded by "plant, company, or department," whichever refers to the auditee. The profile section is intended to be informative to the reader. In some instances, the reader has not had the opportunity to visit the facility of the auditee. The profile section should be designed to be a "stage setter" for the reader. It should help the reader visualize the entity, number of employees, production, or implications of adjustments attributable to company size. The profile, as the situation warrants, may be excluded or contain a narrative description or financial schedules.

The profile should not dominate the report. Instead, it should be limited in size to approximately an informative paragraph. Comparative financial information, if included, should not leave the reader with unanswered questions. Significant variations should be explained.

Keep in mind that the profile should not distract from the purposes of the report, which are the summary, scope, and conclusion sections.

Scope—The scope section has two principal functions. One is to identify exactly what was done during the audit and the second is, to delineate in writing that which was not done.

The scope should clearly state the work that was limited to or restricted to the payroll system, as an example. If internal controls were reviewed on certain systems, but not others, it must be clearly indicated. A general statement such as, "we reviewed the plant's systems of internal controls," is not specific to the reader and leaves the audit open for criticism later. To state "certain" systems were reviewed is better, but not as good as indicating that specific systems such as payroll, accounts payable, and accounts receivable systems were not reviewed. Clearly stating what was done in the audit leaves no doubt as to what was not done. In certain situations, it may be necessary to clearly qualify the scope section by saying "we did not review, test, etc."

Conclusion—The conclusions can only be written on the basis of the work performed in the scope section and subject to the major exceptions contained in the summary section.

No new or additional information can be interjected into the conclusion which has not been specifically stated in these two areas (Scope and Summary).

We should conclude or state our opinion on the fairness of the account balances, financial statements, the adequacy of internal controls, or the reliability of systems, etc.

SAM POLE COMPANY	(LOGO)	CORPORATE AUDIT DEPARTMENT	
		PROCEDURES MANUAL	DATE:

TITLE: Corporate Audit Report Process	NO: 4.1	PAGES:

Figure 4.8 Lead Paragraph Example

This report summarizes the significant results of our interim audit of the company's accounting records and selected internal control procedures. Detailed recommendations and comments, after review with company's management, were provided to the Controller for written response to this office and to other key officials and the Public Accountants for their information.

Summary—The summary component summarizes the detailed recommendations and comments section of the report. The detailed recommendations and comments section does not accompany the audit report issued to the Audit Committee. Therefore, the summary never contains information not published in the detailed recommendations and comments section.

Of the five attributes that are used as a basis for writing a recommendation, only a statement of condition and a statement of action are used to write the points of the summary.

The summary only includes major or material exceptions resulting from the audit. Considerable thought should be given to what is included in the summary and, second, to how it is written. Problems may arise if the auditor overreacts or improperly states the situation. Therefore, the summary may indicate that an audit disclosed no material weaknesses.

Other recommendations and comments not considered material should be addressed in the summary by referring to them in total as one item covered by a few sentences.

Statement of action to summary items may either be included with the summary items individually or prepared in a trailing paragraph to the last summary item.

Discussion items may be included in the summary if material. Since discussion items written with the same attributes as recommendations, the statement of condition and statement of action will be included.

A discussion item is generally only used when the auditee objects to a recommendation on the grouds that they have no control over the subject. If we feel strongly the item should be included in the report, the discussion item approach is a way around the situation. The discussion items do not require a response from the auditee, but still communicate the problem to management and the Audit Committee.

Examples of summary items are as follows:

- Accrued payroll was understated $1 million at December 31. It was recommended that management investigate and adjust the account. This account was adjusted January 7, 19xx.

- Contract terms covering sales of real estate should be reviewed by counsel and entires properly recorded in accordance with GAAP.

- Fifty thousand dollars was lost due to weak internal controls in the data-processing area. We recommended system changes to help prevent future occurrences.

Manager's Signature—The Audit Manager is responsibile for the review and signing of the audit report issued to the Audit Committee of the Board of Directors. He may assign this responsibility to others under certain circumstances.

Distribution—The distribution is a multistep process. After the report is written in draft form, a copy is sent to the Director of Auditing and the auditee simultaneously. A specially designed cover letter is used to convey the drafts to the auditee. This cover letter indicates the draft has been sent to the auditee first for comments and that time is of the essence.

The second step toward distribution, after review and corrections are accomplished, is to send the draft to the Corporate Controller and Director of Auditing, or the next level of authority over the auditee.

After the drafts clear the second step and adjustments or corrections are made, it may be necessary to send a copy to the auditee and Director of Auditing, a second time. But, pending this situation, the report is ready for distribution. Standard distributions for the report consist of:

Sam Pole Company
Audit Committee
Chief Operating Officer

Company Level
Director of Auditing
Chief Financial Officer

Division/Branch/Department
(as applicable)
Comptroller
Chief Accountant, etc.

Public Accounting Firm
Partner
Manager

II. In-depth Recommendations and Comments—Detail

This section is issued with the audit report, but is not distributed to everyone on the distribution list. See distribution of the audit report in a prior section. Because this section may become separated from the audit report, it must be written to stand alone as an independent document. Figure 4.10 "Corporate Audit Detail Recommendations and Comments" presents an example of this report.

Cover page—An optional cover page may be developed to separate the audit report from the detailed recommendations and comments section. If you elect to insert this page, it could contain "Detailed Recommendations and Comments" as a title and be centered on the page.

Heading—The heading consists of the auditee name, the name of the section, "Corporate Audit Detailed Recommendations and Comments" and the "as of" date of the audit.

Lead paragraph—The purpose of the lead or introduction paragraph is to convey to the reader three points. The first point is that this document supplements our summary audit report to the Audit Committee. Second, there is a summarized restatement of our conclusion. Finally, a written response is required. An example follows:

"These detailed recommendations and comments supplement our summary audit report to the Audit Committee of the Board of Directors in which we concluded that internal controls for the payroll and account balances were fairly stated in all material respects as of April 30, 19xx. These detailed recommendations and comments were reviewed with appropriate levels of branch management and are subject to their written response in accordance with corporate policy."

Categories—For purposes of organization, subtitles are used to group recommendations and comments relating to the same subject, i.e., all recommendations and comments relating to accounts payable should be numbered under the subtitle accounts payable.

The subtitles are typed on the left margin in bold type and underlined. To emphasize the subtitle, double spacing is used before and after the subtitle.

The numbering sequence starts with the first recommendation and is continuous to the last recommendation under that subtitle. Numbers start over under each subtitle.

Recommendations—We have chosen to use recommendations rather than findings to describe the audit exceptions because it has a more positive connotation. Recommendations are one of the five attributes that make up a finding, as published by the Institute of Internal Auditors.

In lieu of saying "these are our findings," inferring we found something wrong, we present a more positive image by saying "These are our recommendations for improvement." We do not say that anything was wrong, merely that you can improve.

In addition, it implies the professionalism of auditors in improving the auditee's problems as opposed to dwelling or publishing their problems and failings.

Comments—Comments differ from recommendations in that the five attributes are not present: condition, criteria, effect, cause, and recommendation. Comments are more of a remark or brief statements of fact or opinion. To lessen the confusion, the attribute recommendation has also been renamed statement of action. Care should be used in that generally, anything material enough for the report should be adequately supported.

Discussion Items—Discussion items are developed and written as recommendations, but differ in that the auditee is not required to respond to these items. Discussion items are used in instances where the auditee objects to an item being included in his or/her report when he or she is not directly responsible for the situation. The auditors feel strongly that the situation needs the exposure in a written report. A compromise is the discussion item approach, which could be used only as a last resort.

Manager's Signature—The manager is responsible for signing the recommendation and comments section.

Exhibits—The exhibit section is optional, but should be considered if additional information will help make your recommendations and comments clear to the auditee or management.

Exhibits may take the form of photographs, flowcharts, financial schedules, adjustment schedules, or other sundry schedules of supporting information. Like pictures, exhibits, are worth a thousand words. Supporting exhibits not only add clarity, but if properly done, add a degree of professionalism to your work.

(e) Open Audit Results and Comments

A task listing will be prepared containing all open audit issues and comments on date of implementation. This will be used to monitor the implementation of audit comments. Periodically, management will be queried on the status of open issues. Follow-up compliance audits will take place one year after the date of the audit, and these task lists will be updated and, in most instances, closed out.

Figure 4.9   Corporate Audit Report

Company Location:	
Audit Date:	Audit Manager:
Date Completed:	Audit Office:
Auditors:	
	Date of Report:

The Audit Committee
Sam Pole Company

This report summarizes the results of our audit of the company's accounting records and selected internal control procedures. Detailed recommendations and comments, after review with local management, were provided to the local accounting personnel for written response to this office, and to other key officials, and to the Public Accountants for their information.

Sam Pole Company Profile

The manufacturing plant produces approximately XXX square yards of carpet tile per month. Comparative operating data are as follows:

	1989	1990
Sales	xxxx	xxxx
Cost of Sales	xxxx	xxxx
Inventory	xxx	xxx
Sales		
Backlog	xxx	xxx
Number of Employees	xx	X

Figure 4.9 Continued

Scope of Audit

Our examination included a review and evaluation of accounting systems, internal control procedures, and tests of account balances.

Conclusion

In our opinion, internal controls are adequate and account balances, as adjusted, are fairly stated in all material respects. Quantities of inventory on hand December 31, 199X, are fairly stated. Weaknesses outlined in the detailed recommendations and comments provided to local management did not have a material effect on the account balances at December 31, 199X.

Summary

The significant matters discussed in the detailed report include the following:

- A Disaster Recovery Plan should be developed for the data processing operation

- Procedures to ensure that computer program changes are properly authorized should be developed

- Documentation for significant computer applications is weak and should be improved.

Manager
Internal Audit Department

Distribution:
Headquarters
President
Chief Financial Officer
Local President
Local Accountant

Figure 4.10   Corporate Audit Detail Recommendations and Comments

SAM POLE COMPANY

CORPORATE AUDIT
RECOMMENDATIONS & COMMENTS

December 31, 199x

These detailed recommendations and comments supplement our report to the Audit Committee, in which we concluded that account balances as adjusted were fairly stated in all material respects and controls were adequate at December 31, 19XX. These detailed recommendations and comments were reviewed with appropriate levels of management and, in accordance with corporate policy, are subject to their written response.

Disaster Recovery

In the event of emergency or disaster in which the System 38 is not available for long-term use, there are no contingency plans in effect for the continuance of processing on the System 38. This could result in a delay of processing transactions and have an adverse effect on business operations.

Recommendations/Comments

We recommend that management initiate efforts to develop a disaster recovery plan. In the event that the System 38 is disabled, contingency plans would then be in place to allow continued processing at an off-site facility. A disaster recovery plan should meet the following criteria:

- To identify a location for further processing. This could be a cold site in which a third party has another System 38 which BITS would have access to, or an arrangement with IBM that would permit them to be provided with another System 38 on short notice
- A list of contacts in the event of emergency
- A list of programs and data files needed for recovery
- Detailed instructions on execution of plan.

Figure 4.10 Continued

Program Change Control

Program change control is not formally addressed. Requests for changes to programs should be authorized by user departments. To be properly controlled, a formal authorization form should be developed, indicating the reason for the change, user approval to initiate the project, and final sign-off. Only properly authorized, changed programs should be placed into production libraries.

Recommendation

All program change requests should be properly authorized in writing by the manager or supervisor of the user departments. When the program change has been made, the manager or supervisor of the user department should sign the program change form, signifying that the program has been changed according to the original instructions. The program change form should then be filed in numerical sequence. A copy of the program change form should also be filed with the system's documentation such that a record of each change made to the system is kept in chronological sequence.

Documentation

Good documentation of computerized applications is necessary to document the methods and formulas utilized in the computer operation, to provide a tool to train new personnel, to provide operators with instructions and to assist programmers with systems development and program modification work.

We believe documentation is an important area and should be implemented. This may require management support for the development of a plan to document systems by certain key target dates. We suggest that documentation along the following lines be considered:

- **System documentation includes:**
  Systems description
  System flowcharts, showing the flow of data through the system and the relationship between processing and computer steps
  Input descriptions
  Output descriptions
  File descriptions
  Copies of authorizations and their effective dates for system changes that have been implemented.

Figure 4.10 Continued

- **Program documentation consists of:**
  Brief narrative description
  Flowcharts
  Sources statements or parameter listings
  Control features
  File formats and record layouts
  Record of program changes
  Input/output formats
  Operating instructions.

- **Operations documentation includes:**
  Descriptions of functions
  Inputs and outputs
  Sequence of cards, tapes, disks, and files
  Setup instructions and operating system requirements
  Operating notes listing program messages, halts, and action to signal the end of jobs
  Control procedures to be performed by operations
  Recovery and restart procedures
  Estimated normal and maximum run-time
  Instructions to the operator in the event of an emergency.

- **User documentation consists of:**
  Description of the system
  Error correction procedures
  List of control procedures and an indication of who is responsible for performing those procedures
  Cutoff procedures for submission of data to the data processing department
  Description of how the user department should check reports for accuracy
  Application analyst support (i.e., name of contact)
  Impact on operations (i.e., resources consumed, response time, turn-around time, elapsed time, manual labor time, user training/impact
  Testing plan (i.e., individuals responsible and titles, testing schedule, test results)
  Authorization (i.e., data center approval, programmer and project manager, quality assurance, and user aproval)
  A log to permit the tracing of transmittals through the change control cycle.

Figure 4.10 Continued

- **Establishment of formal testing procedures to include:**
    Identification of the person responsible
    When the test will take place/begin
    When the test will be completed
    Details of the test
    Actual results of the test
    Approval of test results by the data center, programmer, and user.

MANAGER
—INTERNAL AUDIT DEPARTMENT

4.2 REPORT TO MANAGEMENT

The report to management should summarize the activities of the department in the interim since the last report to management. These activities should include audits performed and planned or changes made to plans. All department administrative activities including quality assurance, personal development programs, and participation in other company sponsored programs should be considered. The report should be prepared on a detailed basis prior to the next scheduled audit committee meeting. This will enable you to inform management of some of the items that will be included in the administrative section of your report to the audit committee. It will also enable you to integrate the text of this material into the audit committee report to save work when that report is being developed.

Communications with management is a very important element of an internal audit function. It is more important than in some other operations because the management issues and output of the audit function are more qualitative than quantitative. In a manufacturing or distribution operation, one can measure the output in units and analyze it in many ways. Audit functons have a lot of control over the quantity and quality of the work they perform. However, it is difficult for management to understand the issues involved in running a successful audit function and producing quality audit reports. Audit management has a number of opportunities to express their issues and report on activities. The formal process involves issuing audit reports (Section 4.1) and issuing reports to the Audit Committee (Section 4.3). In this section, we deal with the opportunity to report on a somewhat more detailed basis to management.

As noted earlier in this section, if possible, the Report to Management should be prepared prior to Audit Committee meetings. This is so that the material developed for this report can be reworked for inclusion in the report to the Audit Committee. There are no formal guidelines for what should be included in the Report to Management. Therefore, wide latitude should be used to help explain issues and promote progress achieved within the audit operation. Figure 4.11 is an example of a Report to Management. The format is simple and self-explanatory. However, great care should be taken to include all relevant activities on a prospective basis, as well as activities that have already taken place. In order to demonstrate the tone and range a Report to Management can take, a number of sample report elements have been included. In addition, the report could be patterned to other similar reports required within your organization. Some of the sections that you should consider including are: (a) Corporate Order Department personnel issues; (b) activities related to the external accounting firm; (c) education; (d) internal audit reports issued, pending and in process; (e) budget status.

The Report to Management should be addressed to the Management reporting line of the Chief Auditor. This report is generally not copied to the Audit Committee but should be copied to the President or CEO, if appropriate.

Figure 4.11   Report to Management Example

SAM POLE COMPANY

INTEROFFICE CORRESPONDENCE

TO:	Senior Management	OFFICE:	New York
FROM:	Chief Auditor	OFFICE:	New York
SUBJECT:	Internal Audit Status Report	DATE:	September 10, 19xx

This summarizes the department and my activities since the status report dated July 15, 19xx.

BUDGET FOR 19xx

The budget for 19xx has been drafted and will be presented to you and the Audit Committee on schedule. Due to the addition of a Director and an operational audit unit, the total budget will grow beyond normal inflation.

INTERNAL AUDITS

Audit Reports:

We continue to strive for timely report issuance. At this date, we have the following audit report status:

Issued Since July Status Report

> XYZ Susidiary
> Tulane Contract Audit
> Purchasing Department Audit

Figure 4.11   Continued

Pending Issuance

    Transportation Department
    ABC Subsidiary

Physical Inventories:

In cases where reports are to be issued upon completion of location audits, inventory audit findings will also be included. In other cases, only exception reports will be issued regarding observations and review of compilations. We observed these physical inventories since the July status report:

    XYZ Subsidiary
    ABC Subsidiary

    Main Supplies Inventory

ORGANIZATION/PERSONNEL

The department comprised 37 professionals and 2 secretaries at September 1,

	Total	*East*	*West*	*International*
Professionals	35	15	14	6
Secretaries	2	1	1	—
	37	16	15	6

which reflects the termination of John Joe and resignation of Jane Doe in the East and hiring of Pat Plum (CPA–CA) as a semi-senior in the West. We continue to attempt further East staff reduction by transfer to other departments.

To date, the West manager is pleased with the performance of his staff. He is now recruiting for another semi-senior.

Annual performance reviews were discussed with each eligible East staff member in conjunction with salary increases granted effective September 1. The staff generally responded receptively to constructive criticism designed to insist on or encourage, at minimum, competent professional performance. With certain exceptions, staff members considered salary increases equitable.

Figure 4.11 Continued

EDUCATION/TRAINING

Advance Systems, Inc.

Jim will lead a one-day, in-house (September 11 at the East office) videotape-supported orientation program on IS audit concepts, for the East staff. The West staff participated in a similar program on September 8. These in-house seminars are designed to provide basic background and set the tone for maximum benefit from the MPC Institute course.

MPC Institute

The MPC Institute staff will conduct, at their New York offices, a week-long seminar beginning on September 14, for the entire professional staff, concentrating on auditing in a contemporary computer environment. We have also invited Sam Pole personnel from other departments/ locations to join us for some of the more technical sessions dealing with controls, to convey to them emphatically the significance of controls and also to improve their understanding of the auditor's purpose and responsibilities in a computer environment.

Other

In a less formal, yet structured manner, individual staff members are involved with IIA self-study courses dealing with internal audit theory and practice and statistical sampling. This work is monitored by our Personnel Development Coordinator.

In order to enable staff members to prepare for the CPA examinations and still fulfill audit schedule responsibilities, we have arranged with XYZ to use their self-study guides, at no cost to Sam Pole.

MANAGEMENT DEVELOPMENT PROGRAM PARTICIPANTS—OFF-STAFF ASSIGNMENTS

Bill Clark, between audit assignments, will assist the CFO during October in assembling, reviewing and analyzing operating companies' 19xx budget proposals.

We have also offered to assist the Director of Financial Analysis on 19xx budget matters, by making Peter Daily (East) or Rod Prokop (West) available for six weeks to two months.

These opportunities have a two-fold purpose: (1) to broaden participants' exposure and experience in Sam Pole; and (2) to add another dimension in the evaluation process from sources outside internal audit.

	CORPORATE AUDIT DEPARTMENT	
(LOGO)	PROCEDURES MANUAL	DATE:
TITLE: Report to Management	NO: 4.2	PAGES:

Figure 4.11 Continued

We do foresee a potential problem associated with these off-staff assignments. The demand for Management Development Program participants to work outside the department is likely to conflict with our peak workload period—the Fall—when we experience our heaviest external audit coordination commitment. We are developing our audit plans and schedules to attempt effective attainment of both goals.

SPECIAL STAFF ASSIGNMENTS

New Jersey Mill

John Jones continues to assist in the development of a plant cost accounting manual. We have received favorable feedback regarding his contribution. Out of pocket expense and pro rata salary is billed to the plant, relieving department expense.

Atlanta Foundry

At the ADC Division's request, Jane Paul and Marc John were given a two-week assignment to develop overview flow charts of the plant cost accounting system. Having completed a portion of the work, continuing the assignment has been suspended pending agreement on the scope of the work. Out of pocket expenses were billed to ABC.

POLICY STATEMENTS

Compliance Program

Results of circularization for employee acknowledgment of compliance with our code of conduct are virtually complete. Responses received at this office disclosed no conflict or other situations which warrant reporting. We plan to issue a brief formal report on the results of our review.

Policy Statement Booklet

The supply of booklets in New York is exhausted. We have submitted suggested changes to the text of the booklet to the General Council. We also offered to assist them toward publication of the next revision.

Figure 4.11 Continued

OTHER MATTERS

Security

As noted in my prior status reports and memos, we have been working with the Finance Director to assess ways to improve the corporation's focus on security. We are considering the need for centralizing the responsiblity for all aspects of security within the company. Our recommendation was for a high level survey of our current practices and security plans. To further our ground work, we have set up a meeting with the General Council to apprise him of our activities to date and get his input.

Professional Activities

As president of the New York Chapter, ISACA, John Jones presides over monthly board meetings and dinner meetings for members.

On July 24, the Chief Auditor addressed our external audit firm's seminar for internal aduitors on internal audit department practices.

Marc John serves on the IIA Board of Governors and as Chairman of the Editorial Committee.

Jane Paul serves on the IIA International Research Committee.

Regards

4.3 REPORT TO AUDIT COMMITTEE

In addition to the distribution of reports as audits are completed, periodically a summary report will be made to the Audit Committee. This report will include a report on internal controls and summary of items of significance, the summary of the Corporate Audit Department reports and incorporate Audit Department status reports. This report provides the opportunity to explain the accomplishments of the department and should be viewed as a critical Audit Department product. Figure 4.12 presents a sample of a report to the Audit Committee.

Figure 4.12   Report to Audit Committee

Sam Pole Company
100000 Mapole Street East
Flagstaff, AZ 12345

February 28, 19xx

Gentlemen:

I am pleased to present this report to the Audit Committee, comprising:

    I. Report on internal controls
       and summary of items of significance.

    II. Summary of Corporate Audit Department reports.

    III. Corporate Audit Department status report.

Audits in process and concluded since our report dated December XX, 19xx, have not disclosed any developments which require action by the Committee.

I look forward to meeting with you to review the contents of this report and any other matters you may wish to discuss.

Very truly yours,

I. M. Brilliant
Internal Audit Director

SAM POLE COMPANY

Report to the Audit Committee

February 28, 19xx

SECTION I

Report on Internal Controls

Sam Pole Company maintains systems of internal accounting controls and procedures designed to provide reasonable assurance that all transactions are properly recorded in the books and records, that prescribed policies and procedures are adhered to, and that the corporation's assets are protected from unauthorized use.

To date, based on continuing reviews of internal controls at company locations, nothing has come to our attention since our prior report to indicate that the existing systems of internal control are not effective. However, as commented on in our December report, the company must be continually alert, so that the changing conditions in Sam Pole Company's operations, primarily reductions in the number of salaried employees, are not accompanied by a weakening of existing internal controls, more specifically, the segregation of duties. We plan to continually focus on such areas of potential weaknesses and report situations where we believe acation is required.

Summary of Items of Significance

Although we have made recommendations to management to improve internal controls, nothing of a significant nature was disclosed which would require action by the Audit Committee. We have received full cooperation from all levels of management and have been permitted access to all requested company records and documents.

SECTION II

Summary of Corporate Audit Department Reports

The following audit reports, issued since the December 5, 19xx, Audit Committee meeting, are enclosed for your review:

> Corporate Data Center
> Sam Pole Company
> Payroll System
> Products Company
> Sales Company—Trading and Logistics

Recommendations relate to internal controls which can be improved; however, no material exceptions were noted. In the event of significant findings, we would promptly advise the Committee and issue a preliminary report.

Our comments and recommendations have involved matters significant to the organizational units audited. Based on our evaluation of auditee responses, we believe that our recommendations have been or are being given considerable management attention and action.

SECTION III

Audits and Related Activities

Audit Activities

Audits pertinent to annual corporate financial statement reporting centered primarily on completing interim and year end audits under the rotation plan with our external auditors. We also continued our reviews of automated systems, including customer accounts receivable, salaried payroll and accounts payable.

Supplies Inventories

At the December meeting of the Audit Committee, we reported on our management requested special review of supplies inventories. Since our last report . . .

Steering Committee

The Director of Auditing, while not a member, attends by invitation the Information Resource Steering Committee meetings. Briefly this involvement provides input to the Committee and knowledge of company plans to the Director. As a result of attending these meetings we are planning special audit training in the following areas . . .

Disposition Audits

As previously reported, we have been significantly involved in disposition audits of the various units. Most recently, we assisted in the development of data which allowed for timely. . . .

Administrative and Other Matters

Professional Staff

The current field staff, meeting our authorized complement, totals 20; 6 in New York and 14 in Denver (as compared to 19 in 19xx). Our current three-year plan indicates a need for approximately 21 auditors. We will adjust this plan and reevaluate staffing requirements after developing the rotation program (based upon the company's new operating structure) with the public accountants.

High turnover has continued in Denver, due to the company's situation and increased salaries available in an area with a high employment rate. Future recruiting, unless otherwise required, will be at the entry level.

We are pleased to report that we have promoted Mr. Sharp to manager in New York and J. Pink to supervising senior in Detroit. Two individuals transferred from the audit staff; one to the Controller's staff and the other to MIS.

Quality Assurance Program

A responsibility of the Director, as described in the department's charter, is that audit work conform to the Standards for the Professional Practice of Internal Auditing. The Standards call for an independent external review, at least once every three years, to appraise the quality of the department's operations. Accordingly, we have tentatively agreed to reciprocal department reviews with IPL Corporation in 19xx and 19xx. Preliminary discussions will be held in late February, with a review of our department planned for June 19xx.

SAM POLE	(LOGO)	CORPORATE AUDIT DEPARTMENT	
COMPANY		PROCEDURES MANUAL	DATE:

TITLE: Report to Audit Committee	NO: 4.3	PAGES:

We have been planning this independent review of our total department performance for several years. Initially, we had each audit group perform a high-level quality assurance review. In 19xx, we had a more in-depth review in New York and Detroit with a good appraisal (on a test basis) of the adequacy of each other's performance. We are now looking forward to this independent peer review to see how we can improve our operations.

Professional Certification

We have developed a professional certification policy for the internal audit department. We are strongly encouraging certification (CPA, CIA, CMA, etc.) within the first five years or before promotion to senior. We are providing partial company assistance to provide further incentive and yet ensure the individual's own sincere interest. A copy of the policy for your review is enclosed in Appendix XX. (Not shown here; see policies section of the Manual)

Chapter 5

PERSONNEL ADMINISTRATION AND RECRUITING

5.1 PERSONNEL RECRUITING

Internal Audit consists of people and procedures. Talented people following a well-thought-out, tailored methodology will produce consistent quality audit products. We should not lose sight of the support role of audit. Like the accounting department and other important groups in a company, audit does not produce the primary product or service. However, the audit mission (as defined in the audit department charter) is crucial to the company's success, providing independent review and constructive advice.

In order to attract and maintain qualified staff the corporate audit department has put in place a personnel development program (see Section 5.2). However, the selection of the best individuals is the first step in the process.

(a) Sources of Personnel

Internal auditors are typically accountants who have an interest in auditing. In many cases, this interest is combined with a desire to gain a good understanding of many business functions. The audit function exposes auditors to a large number of areas in a company's operations. Therefore, it is considered an excellent training ground. Consequently, some entry-level auditors will consider audit a stepping-stone in their career progression. If the audit department is successful and well respected, a percentage of auditors will choose to remain and progress to audit management positions. Since most organizations, including audit departments, have pyramid structures, these career path issues must be managed effectively to promote audit staff development and progression.

Staff can be obtained from a number of sources, which include the following:

- Direct recruitment from colleges

- Transfers from other company functions

- Outside hires.

(i) Direct recruitment from colleges
To develop a professional-level internal audit program, most functions require a college degree for new hires. Colleges and universities develop students' basic skills and most include an auditing course in the accounting degree program. The first step will be to identify the schools you may want to work with and study their curricula. Most schools have on-campus recruitment programs. Companies that participate in these programs are invited to on-campus recruitment days for interviews with students who have indicated an interest in exploring a career with the company.

Thanks largely to the efforts of the Institute of Internal Auditors model internal audit curriculum program, some colleges have specific programs in internal audit. These students have chosen internal auditing as a specialization and are sought after by companies seeking better qualified graduates.

(ii) Transfers from other company functions

In some cases candidates may be available within the company. Some companies have sophisticated human resource programs that can assist audit management with hiring and career progression issues. Audit functions should always attempt to hire the best possible candidates and never "settle" or accept an individual as an accommodation to another department.

(iii) Outside hires

An excellent source of outside candidates is from public practice. Public accounting firms recruit primarily accounting graduates and, in most cases, provide them with formal hands-on training programs in the early years with the firm. Some also provide industry and computer training. Of course, large internal-audit departments are capable of organizing and providing similar professional development programs. In most cases, however, they cannot provide the diversified experience available in public practice.

(b) Recruitment Aids

Forethought and planning will improve recruiting results. Candidates will be favorably impressed when presented with company structure charts, organization charts, and a schematic of the personnel development program similar to the one presented in the Manual. Some audit departments develop brochures describing function, activities, and benefits (e.g., experience in many company operations, travel and potential career progression). The development of a summary of the current staff with qualifications may also add value. Some departments that encourage career development in the audit department and within the company develop career summaries on current and preceding members of the department.

An interview questionnaire for new internal auditors should be developed and used to summarize interviews and results. Figure 5.1 is a sample form.

(c) Management Development Programs

People can be products, too! Some audit departments develop or participate in management development programs. These programs can involve internal audit as an initial or mid-career step. For instance, new college graduates can be hired by the internal audit department and assigned to other company operations for portions of the year. After two or three years they transfer to another unit after a successful project. This will add work to the audit management function, and it will also create a positive deliverable or product. Such programs would be discussed with senior management and/or the audit committee and added to the audit department function directly in the audit charter.

In some notable examples, personnel development programs have greatly enhanced the reputation of the audit function through the addition of a tangible measureable product: former audit personnel rising to higher level positions in the organization.

Figure 5.1   Interview Questionnaire for New Internal Auditors

NAME _____   DATE _____

SCHOOL _____   INTERVIEW
                                                  APPOINTMENT _____

BACKGROUND

EDUCATION: _____   FAMILY: _____

_____

_____

_____

CAREER HISTORY

_____

_____

_____

_____

_____

LONG-TERM CAREER OBJECTIVE

_____

_____

_____

_____

WHAT YOU ENJOY MOST ABOUT YOUR JOB

_____

_____

_____

Figure 5.1 Continued

KNOWLEDGE OF AND/OR INTEREST IN COMPUTERS

_____

_____

_____

GREATEST ACCOMPLISHMENT IN YOUR CAREER

_____

_____

_____

WHAT IS YOUR APPROACH TO MANAGING PEOPLE?

_____

_____

_____

WHAT DO YOU DO WHEN YOU NEED TO MAKE A CHANGE, AND THERE IS RESISTANCE?

_____

_____

_____

Figure 5.1 Continued

STRENGTHS?

_____

_____

_____

WEAKNESSES?

_____

_____

_____

HOW DO YOU FEEL ABOUT TRAVEL?

_____

_____

_____

UNDERSTANDING OF INTERNAL AUDIT

How do you view the role of the Internal Auditor?

_____

_____

_____

_____

Figure 5.1 Continued

How does it differ from Public Audit?

_____

_____

_____

_____

Should Audit view itself as a business?

_____

_____

_____

_____

Should Audit be a profit center?

_____

_____

_____

_____

Are you familiar with the Institute of Internal Auditors and/or the IS Audit and Control Association?

_____

_____

_____

HOBBIES — AVOCATIONS — OTHER INTERESTS:

_____

_____

_____

Figure 5.1 Continued

CANDIDATE RATING

	LOW		HIGH		COMMENTS

1. Personal Appearance
   (First impression, courtesy, grooming)
   1 2 3 4 _____

2. Communication Skills
   (Vocabulary, grammar, clarity, participation in interview, persuasiveness)
   1 2 3 4 _____

3. Attitude
   (Outlook, mood, responsiveness)
   1 2 3 4 _____

4. Personality and Maturity
   (Friendliness, self-confidence, rapport,
   realistic estimates of value, sense of humor
   1 2 3 4 _____

5. Mental Alertness and Ability
   (Logic, discretion, response to questions,
   inquiring mind, potential for growth)
   1 2 3 4 _____

6. Motivation and Drive
   (Initiative, achievement oriented,
   energy level)
   1 2 3 4 _____

7. Interest
   (In position, breadth of general interest in
   internal audit, knowledge of profession)
   1 2 3 4 _____

8. Leadership Ability
   (Desire to organize and direct, willing-
   ness to accept responsibility)
   1 2 3 4 _____

9. Overall Evaluation
   1 2 3 4 _____

RECOMMENDATION

1. Would you like to have the candidate work with you?   Yes ☐   No ☐

2. Would you recommend the candidate for employment?   Yes ☐   No ☐

Comments _____

_____

_____

_____

_____

INTERVIEWER NAME: _____ LOCATION: _____

SIGNATURE: _____ REVIEWED BY: _____ DATE: _____

(i) Certifications

Certifications, including Certified Public Accountant (CPA), Certified Internal Auditor (CIA), Certified Information Systems Auditor (CISA) and Certified Management Accountant (CMA) are significant personal achievements and provide evidence of basic skill levels and knowledge. They also add to the internal audit function's image. Policies can be developed to encourage staff members to attain certifications, which should be seriously considered in reviewing new-hire qualifications.

5.2 PERSONAL DEVELOPMENT

Internal Auditing consists of quality people employing quality procedures in an independent and proactive manner. In order to sustain the implementation of the most appropriate procedures and to provide for the continuing improvement of the auditors, a professional development program becomes a critical component of the Internal Audit practice.

Consider the following quote from *Future Shock*, by Alvin Toffler:

> If society itself were standing still, there might be little pressure on the individual to update his own supply of images, to bring them in line with the latest knowledge available in society. So long as the society in which he is embedded is stable or slowly changing, the images on which he bases his behavior can also change slowly. But to function in a fast-changing society, to cope with swift and complex change, the individual must turn over his own stock of images at a rate that, in some way, correlates with the pace of change. His model must be updated. To the degree that it lags, his responses to change become inappropriate, he becomes increasingly thwarted, ineffective. Thus, there is intense pressure on the individual to keep up with the generalized pace. Today, change is so swift and relentless in the techno-societies that yesterday's truths suddenly become today's fictions, and the most highly skilled and intelligent members of society admit difficulty in keeping up with the deluge of new knowledge—even in extremely narrow fields.*

(a) Introduction

In order to ensure that the Corporate Audit Department's education plan is implemented, the responsibility for coordination has been assigned to the Manager Policies and Control. As Coordinator of Education, the Manager Policies and Control will assist in the development of the departmental education plan and individual auditors' educational plans. He/she will work closely with the staff and managers to achieve the objectives of the Professional Development Program and report periodically to the Director of Auditing on the status of the program.

(b) Objectives

The Corporate Audit Department Training Program has been designed to improve and maintain the professional competence of the corporate auditors so that they can effectively perform their function to the fullest extent. Additionally, it is intended to provide for personal professional growth and job satisfaction. The program—combined with on-the-job experience and training—and a comprehensive evaluation process, is intended to provide a basis for advancement in the Audit Department, or for potential placement in key financial or general management positions within the company.

Future Shock, Alvin Toffler, Bantam Book, August 1971.

Every professional has a responsibility to maintain and advance his or her basic skills. The program is intended to provide a vehicle for the individual to accomplish this requirement. The program will be as successful for you as you make it. Additionally, to develop strong business acumen, daily reading of the general financial press is essential. Auditors are generalists, to a large degree, and should always be cognizant of current trends in business and finance, to ascertain the importance, if any, on their audit assignment.

(c) Coordinator of Education

- Assists the Director and audit managers in surveying staff and analyzing training needs

- Recommends comprehensive, systematic training program for the Corporate Audit Department

- Coordinates the training activities for corporate auditors and makes staff aware of all training opportunities

- Assists auditors in developing individual goals and training programs

- Develops and implements evaluation programs for all training activities involving internal audit

- Investigates specific training programs as requested by other members of the staff and authorized by the Director of Auditing

- Assists in the evaluation of training programs and reviews regular (quarterly) training reports on staff members for the Director of Auditing

- Develops policies and procedures for maintaining and using the staff library. Assures audit management that the library is adequately stocked and keeps staff informed of new acquisitions pertinent to their particular needs.

(d) Corporate Audit Training Model

The corporate audit training model (Figure 5.2) includes a structured approach to core training critical for first- and second-year auditors. The model goes on to suggest a training program for auditors beyond the basic core programs. These are labeled as "advanced," for third year and after.

The core of the Corporate Audit Program is on-the-job training through effective supervision and constructive evaluations covering areas of need. The program is twofold: the Core Program covering new auditors, and the Advanced, covering education for career-minded internal auditors for periods beyond two years.

Figure 5.2 Overview of Corporate Audit Training Model

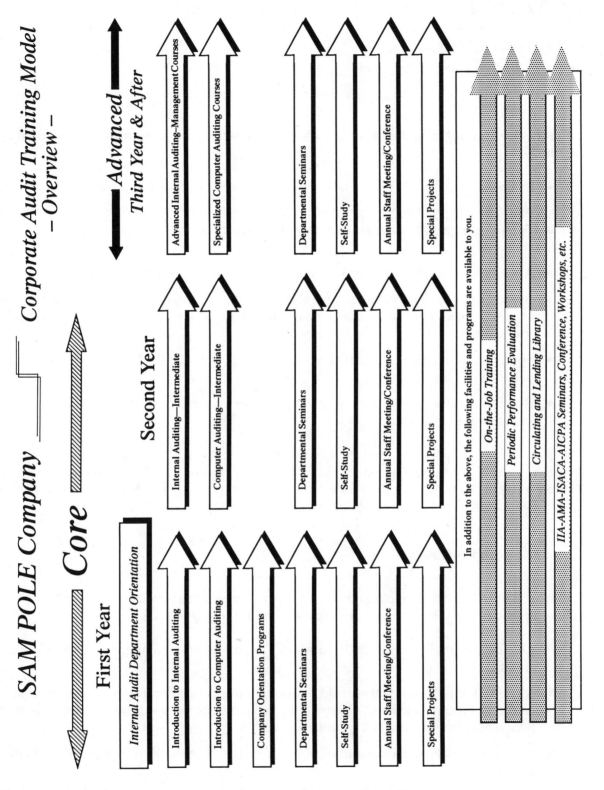

SAM POLE Company   Corporate Audit Training Model
– Overview –

Core

First Year

Internal Audit Department Orientation

Introduction to Internal Auditing

Introduction to Computer Auditing

Company Orientation Programs

Departmental Seminars

Self-Study

Annual Staff Meeting/Conference

Special Projects

Second Year

Internal Auditing—Intermediate

Computer Auditing—Intermediate

Departmental Seminars

Self-Study

Annual Staff Meeting/Conference

Special Projects

Advanced
Third Year & After

Advanced Internal Auditing–Management Courses

Specialized Computer Auditing Courses

Departmental Seminars

Self-Study

Annual Staff Meeting/Conference

Special Projects

In addition to the above, the following facilities and programs are available to you.

On-the-Job Training

Periodic Performance Evaluation

Circulating and Lending Library

IIA-AMA-ISACA-AICPA Seminars, Conference, Workshops, etc.

On-the-job training is supplemented with the following types of formal and informal education:

- In-house seminars and self-study training through the use of audio and visual training courses

- Teaching or speaking engagements to help broaden one's knowledge and communications skills

- Attendance at various outside seminars, workshops, lectures, and conferences, etc.

- Availability of a library of texts and reference materials covering internal auditing, as well as specific areas of business management, taxation, finance, purchasing, construction contracts, etc.

- Specialized courses, when available and/or practical, specially designed to meet the internal auditor's needs

- Routing of selected educational material to the internal audit staff to maintain current knowledge in the field.

The Core Program requires a minimum of two weeks, or eighty hours, per year of formal education or teaching. The Advanced Program requires a minimum of one week, or forty hours, per year. These minimum requirements do not include self-study courses, outside professional meetings, on-the-job training, research, and the use of the library.

(e) Core Program

First Year:

During the first year of employment, attendance at various structured courses is required. The following schedule will be followed, interfaced with on-the-job training:

- All new hires will attend an orientation program on the company and the Corporate Audit Department

- All entry-level auditors will attend a one- to two-week course on Introduction to Corporate Auditing Procedures. This subject could be administered in-house by experienced corporate auditors, or provided by outside trainers

- All auditors will attend at a minimum a five-day Introduction to Computer Auditing course

- Audio/visual courses on audit-related topics will be suggested during the year, and be attended by all staff members

- Mandatory attendance at all staff meetings and in-house internal audit seminars on a regional and centralized basis.

Second Year:

The training program will continue into subsequent years and by the end of the second year, the following should have been attained:

- Continuation of Corporate Auditing procedures at the Intermediate Level as well as attendance at courses relating to the evaluation of internal controls

- Attendance at an in-house or outside seminar on advanced computer audit techniques, or software

- Participation in audio/visual courses on specific topics to be announced, i.e. systems auditing, statistical sampling

- Attendance at in-house Corporate Audit seminars (one week) and regularly scheduled staff meetings.

(f) Advanced Program

The Advanced Program will involve specific tailoring to meet each individual's development needs. As the internal auditor's career progresses, decisions need to be made as to the individual's long-term objectives. If those objectives lie in the internal audit area, provision should be made for the attendance at internal audit management training and conferences. There may be a need for auditors to develop specific skills further. For instance, operational auditing or EDP auditing skills may be required by the department, and/or requested by the individual in their career planning meetings. The professional development program can be tailored for each individual, to help meet departmental, as well as individual, goals.

Included in the advanced stage of the program is an anticipation that the staff member will increase his or her involvement with professional organizations such as the IIA, AICPA, AMA, ISACA, and participate in their educational programs. Staff members, at this level, should be strongly encouraged to develop their own expertise in specific areas and provide training courses to these organizations. Committee assignments can, in some cases, be considered as continuing education endeavors. These decisions must be made by audit management, and documented in the individual's professional development plan.

(g) Record-Keeping

Each auditor is responsible for maintaining a chronological record of his/her training or educational accomplishments while on the Corporate Audit staff. This record will be forwarded quarterly to the Coordinator of Education (see Figure 5.3 Continuing Professional Education [CPE] Record).

SAM POLE
COMPANY

LOGO

CORPORATE AUDIT DEPARTMENT

PROCEDURES MANUAL

DATE:

TITLE: Personal Development

NO: 5.2

PAGES:

Figure 5.3   Continuing Professional Education (CPE) Record

Dates Attended	Name of Course(s)	Presented by Organization/Location	Number of Hours Attended	Course Content or Outline Attached? (Yes/No)	Hours as Instructor	
					Preparation	Teaching

FORM CPE—1

The coordinator will review the forms quarterly and submit them to the Director of Auditing for inclusion in each auditor's personnel file. Certain continuing education credits needed to maintain various professional certifications should be pursued by each individual auditor and will be retained in his or her personnel file.

Performance evaluations will be conducted after each assignment or periodically by each level of supervision, and also placed in the file, so that needs analysis can be made to determine what additional education is required to maintain each staff member's proficiency.

Training records will be used as a reference in scheduling staff members to various assignments. These assignments will help reinforce the retention of course curriculum obtained from the training programs. The Director and audit managers will periodically assess the auditor's training needs, using the CPE record and/or the section on development needs as shown on the performance evaluations. After training assessments are made, both individual and staff training goals and programs will be further developed as required.

The results of this training program should improve the professional competence of all staff members, thus providing the knowledge to function and cope with our fast-changing, complex environment.

SAM POLE COMPANY	LOGO	CORPORATE AUDIT DEPARTMENT	
		PROCEDURES MANUAL	DATE:
TITLE: Personnel Files		NO: 5.3	PAGES:

5.3 PERSONNEL FILES

In order to properly manage the audit profession's department, personnel files will be maintained. Audit department personnel files should be multi-partition files and include, but not be limited to:

1. Employee resume and a copy of the original Company application (if appropriate).

2. Periodic performance appraisals.

3. Summary of salary history and promotions.

4. Corporate Audit Department Background Information Form (Figure 5.4).

5. Corporate Audit Department Interest Questionnaire (Figure 5.5).

These files may be maintained by the Human Resources function. To facilitate the development and maintenance of these departmental files and facilitate the gathering of specific information necessary to proactively manage the corporate audit function, two departmental forms should be completed by all employees and updated annually. These forms are:

Corporate Audit Department Background Information Form

Corporate Audit Department Interest Questionnaire

(a) Corporate Audit Department Background Information Form

This form (Figure 5.4) facilitates two-way communications and helps standardized the basic information required for each employee. The form should be kept in the inside cover of each personnel file. The form also serves to reinforce interest in certifications and professional activities and provides a feedback mechanism for information related to these activities.

(b) Corporate Audit Department Interest Questionnaire

The Corporate Audit Department Interest Questionnaire expands on the Corporate Audit Department Background Information Form by requesting additional information related to the audit professional's preferences. Not all preferences can be granted, but in some cases preferences can be considered in planning.

Figure 5.4 Corporate Audit Department Background Information Form

PERSONAL: Name _____   Telephone # ( ) _____

Address _____   Marital Status _____ _____

_____   No. of Dependents _____
(zip code)

Name of Spouse _____   Children's Names _____

_____

Date of hire _____   Commencement date in IA Dept.

(if different than hire date)

_____

Who to notify in case of emergency:

Name _____   Telephone # ( ) _____

Address _____   Relationship _____

_____
(zip code)

What foreign language(s) do you speak and/or write *fluently*?

_____

CERTIFICATIONS:	Certification	Conferring Organization or State	Date
	_____	_____	_____
	_____	_____	_____
	_____	_____	_____

Figure 5.4 Continued

EDUCATION:

College/University	Attended		Major	Degree
	From	To		
_____	_____	_____	_____	_____
_____	_____	_____	_____	_____
_____	_____	_____	_____	_____

Other Education	Dates	Topic
_____	_____	_____
_____	_____	_____
_____	_____	_____
_____	_____	_____

MEMBERSHIPS:

Professional or Civic Organizations	Dates	Position Held
_____	_____	_____
_____	_____	_____
_____	_____	_____

EDP: Experience in EDP—List college courses and describe any outside experience.

_____

_____

_____

_____

Figure 5.5 Corporate Audit Department Interest Questionnaire

NAME _____ DATE _____

NICKNAME _____

TRAVEL: Percentage of time you prefer to travel out-of-town _____ %; Outside USA _____ %

Do you have access to an automobile for business? Yes _____ No _____

Do you have the required automobile insurance coverage?
($100/300,000 liability and $50,000 property damage)
Yes _____ No _____

EDUCATION: Do you plan outside school attendance during the coming year? Yes _____ No _____

If yes, explain _____

Do you plan to take a professional certification review course during the coming year?
Yes _____ No _____ (Identify) _____

INTERESTS AND PREFERENCES:	STRONG INTEREST	WOULD CONSIDER	NO INTEREST
Interest in participating in:			
Development of in-house educational programs	_____	_____	_____
Instructing in-house education programs	_____	_____	_____
Administrative projects	_____	_____	_____
Professional organization activities	_____	_____	_____
Financial audits	_____	_____	_____
Operational audits	_____	_____	_____
EDP audits	_____	_____	_____
Special projects—audit	_____	_____	_____
Special projects—non-audit	_____	_____	_____

Figure 5.5 Continued

INTERESTS AND PREFERENCES:	STRONG INTEREST	WOULD CONSIDER	NO INTEREST

Interest in transferring to:

Other New York departments
(if yes, indicate department preference, if any)

_____   _____ _____ _____

Other locations
(if yes, indicate company or area of preference, if any)

_____   _____ _____ _____

List below the types of outside or in-house education you would be interested in:

_____
_____
_____
_____

List the courses or topics you might be willing to teach in an in-house program. (Assuming adequate preparation time would be provided):

_____
_____
_____
_____

List below the types of experience and/or specific audit areas in which you would like to or need to broaden your experience.

_____
_____
_____
_____

Comments and/or recommendations:

_____
_____
_____
_____

5.4 PERIODIC PERFORMANCE EVALUATION REVIEW

Periodic performance evaluation is an essential part of our personnel development program. It is expected that all staff members will become familiar with and understand the reporting requirements and instructive guidelines. Staff evaluations, prepared accordingly, can then be expected to be fair and objective appraisals of the person's performance. It cannot emphasize too strongly the importance of timely, constructive interim feedback by the supervisor. Such feedback will help to shape the end-of-assignment evaluation and will expedite its completion and review in the shortest time. The Performance Evaluation Review report is included in Figure 5.6. The report is to be prepared for staff personnel by the in-charge senior or manager promptly at the end of the assignment.

(a) Performance Evaluation Review Guidelines for Preparation of Report

(i) Introduction

Continuous and timely review and evaluation of performance is essential to effective personnel development. To provide for that continuity, the Performance Review report should be prepared promptly by the auditor's supervisor at the end of each assignment. The evaluation should be discussed with the auditor in a constructive manner to encourage continuing efforts toward improvement in performance and the elimination of shortcomings.

The completed report, signed both by the preparer and the person evaluated, will document the:

1. accurate, complete record of the auditor's performance;

2. notification of observed strengths and weaknesses

3. basis for assessing training and development needs (correlated with the auditor's departmental training record),

4. basis for appraisal toward promotion or for transfer, salary review and warning or other administrative action.

The periodic, end of assignment review should be reinforced through effective interim oral or written feedback by the supervisor during the assignment. Interim feedback is the continual process, an integral part of the supervisor's functions. Failure to provide timely feedback is a weakness in the supervisor's performance. The interim performance discussion should provide analysis of both strengths and areas for improvement, emphasizing constructive actions for improving performance. Although interim evaluations need not be in writing, the evaluation form can serve as a checklist for areas to be considered and for notes, as both a basis for that evaluation and a reference point for the end of assignment evaluation.

Figure 5.6   Performance Evaluation Review Form

SAM POLE COMPANY   **PERFORMANCE EVALUATION REVIEW**

Internal Audit Department   **Confidential**

This form is to be prepared for staff personnel by the in-charge senior or manager at the end of each assignment of two weeks or longer. For shorter assignments use your judgment. The COMMENTS SECTION should be completed for all items requested. Comments should be complete and specific, with examples where informative. Reports should be prepared, reviewed and submitted to the Manager, Internal Audit upon completion of the individual's work on the assignment. All personnel reports require Director approval. The personnel report is not a substitute for periodic on-the-job review of performance.

Name: _____   Years at Sam Pole _____   Assignment: _____

Periods: From _____ To _____   From _____ To _____   Number of hours _____

At what level was individual used on this assignment?

☐ Supervising Senior   ☐ Semi-Senior   ☐ Intern   Number of   Number of prior
                                                                                          persons   assignments this
☐ Senior   ☐ Staff Auditor   ☐ Other _____   supervised _____   audit _____

Describe the individual's areas of responsibility. Comment on difficulty of Accounting and Auditing. Describe the cooperation and competence of auditee personnel.

_____
_____
_____
_____
_____
_____
_____
_____
_____
_____
_____

Did the individual receive an oral interim on-the-job review of performance?   ☐ Yes   ☐ No

Did the auditee make any observations about this individual?   ☐ Yes   ☐ No

If yes, discuss, including evaluation of source, in Comments Section

SAM POLE
COMPANY

(LOGO)

CORPORATE AUDIT DEPARTMENT

PROCEDURES MANUAL

DATE:

TITLE: Periodic Performance Evaluation Review | NO: 5.4 | PAGES:

Figure 5.6 Continued

| In reviewing this report, did the individual with your evaluation? Comment, if necessary. | ☐ Agree | ☐ Generally agree | ☐ Disagree |

_____
_____
_____
_____
_____

	Signature of Staff Person	Manager/ Supervisor	Director
Prepared by _____	Evaluated _____	Approval _____	Approval _____
Date _____	Date _____	Date _____	Date _____

COMMENTS SECTION

QUALIFICATIONS FOR COMPETENT PROFESSIONAL PERFORMANCE

The qualifications enumerated in each major qualifications category describe "Competent Professional Performance" which is the effectiveness level required for normal advancement to senior or manager responsibilities. They constitute expected standards of performance. Experience level should be considered in evaluating an individual's performance. Effectiveness levels, <u>as defined on last page</u>, should be indicated for qualifications enumerated in each major qualification. OUTSTANDING and UNSATISFACTORY should be clearly explained.

(Use abbreviations: O; CPP; IN; U; N.)

TECHNICAL SKILLS

• Possesses good working knowledge of the requirements of the work assigned, including but not limited to GAAP, auditing procedures, tax aspects of accounting, EDP auditing techniques.

• Applies good judgment in selection and implementation of audit procedures.

• Applies technical knowledge practically in assigned situations.

• Prepares and causes others to prepare accurate, meaningful, logical, neat, well-referenced working papers.

• Competently develops sound conclusions and explanations.

• Keeps abreast of current technical developments.

_____
_____
_____
_____
_____

Figure 5.6 Continued

ANALYTICAL ABILITIES

- Identifies the significant problems that must be resolved and acquires sufficient objective facts relevant to the problems.

- Properly thinks through problems; formulates accurate findings.

- Is creative, yet pragmatic in posing solutions; does not overly rely on prior experiences.

- Visualizes and presents alternative approaches, but is decisive in making recommendations.

COMMUNICATION SKILLS

- Makes clear and effective oral presentations, formal or informal.

- Writes clearly and concisely with good organization.

- Is persuasive.

- Strives for effective liaison between assistants, other staff, management, auditee.

- Prepares appropriate memoranda for work papers or management awareness.

EFFECTIVE ASSIGNMENT AND RESOURCES MANAGEMENT

- Plans, organizes and controls time and that of assistants.
- Realistically budgets assignment and accomplishes the work within established budgets.
- Effectively delegates work; properly utilizes and supervises assistants.
- Keeps supervisors informed of significant developments, including budget overruns, on a timely basis
- Completes the assignment timely, including final clean-up of details and loose ends.

Figure 5.6 Continued

DEVELOPMENT OF ASSISTANTS – Component professional performance requires timely interim performance feedback to assistants and end-of-assignment evaluations.

- Considers assistants' experience and interests and attempts to vary assignment to help them develop professionally.
- Helps assistants establish work objectives (scope of work, assignment of individual responsibilities, establishment of check points and deadlines, determination of time budgets, etc.) at beginning of assignment.
- Motivates assistants/associates to action.
- Requires quality work from assistants and is effective in reviewing and supervising their work.
- Effectively discusses performance and development with assistants to gain their understanding, acceptance and commitment to improvement, both during and at the completion of the engagement.

PERSONAL ATTRIBUTES

- Evidences self motivation; wants to learn; reaches for responsibility; is enthusiastic, teachable and persevering.
- Evidences leadership; maturity; adaptability to change and new conditions.
- Maintains objectivity and integrity; consistently promotes high professional standards.
- Evidences self-assurance and poise; understanding of people; cooperative attitude.
- Exhibits professional appearance and manner; representative of corporate management.

AUDITEE RELATIONS

- Understands company's business and published policies and procedures.
- Identifies situations with audit potential.
- Develops auditee respect and rapport, without sacrificing independence.
- Demonstrates responsiveness to management needs.

Figure 5.6 Continued

STRENGTHS/WEAKNESSES

• Significant strengths _____
_____
_____

• Weaknesses (correlate with Developmental Need)
_____
_____

DEVELOPMENTAL NEEDS

• Job assignments to: optimize use of talents; provide appropriate broadening experiences; capitalize on individual's interests.

• Training activities and development experiences to help individual perform better in present capacity and prepare for future assignments.
_____
_____
_____

MANAGER/DIRECTOR COMMENTS

• Include here basis for approval of review and any other significant comments.
_____
_____

Figure 5.6 Continued

SUMMARY EVALUATION SECTION

Major Qualification Categories	EFFECTIVENESS LEVEL				
	Out-standing	Competent professional performance	Improve-ment needed	Unsatis-factory	No basis for judgment
• Technical skills	☐	☐	☐	☐	☐
• Analytical abilities	☐	☐	☐	☐	☐
• Communication skills	☐	☐	☐	☐	☐
• Effective assignment and resources management	☐	☐	☐	☐	☐
• Auditee relations	☐	☐	☐	☐	☐
• Development of assistants	☐	☐	☐	☐	☐
• Personal attributes	☐	☐	☐	☐	☐

EFFECTIVENESS LEVELS:

Effectiveness level rating should be based on an individual's performance measured against a standard of normally expected performance for staff at his or her level. The qualifications cited should not be as stringently applied to less experienced personnel. Each effectiveness level rating is defined as follows:

    0 – Outstanding—clearly exceeds the normally expected competent professional performance level. Denotes an exceptional strength.

  CPP – Competent professional performance—meets the qualification as described. Implies a standard of performance usually expected of those advancing normally to senior or manager.

   IN – Improvement needed—indicates inconsistent performance or performance which falls short of that normally expected. Implies the capability for improvement given additional experience, education, etc.

    U – Unsatisfactory—indicates unacceptable performance. It may result from a poor attitude, lack of ability, etc.

    N – No basis for judgment—should be used when the individual did not have the opportunity to demonstrate the qualification in question.

Ratings other than these should not be used. A choice must be made as to which rating is most appropriate. Written comments should explain borderline decisions.

SAM POLE COMPANY	(LOGO)	CORPORATE AUDIT DEPARTMENT	
		PROCEDURES MANUAL	DATE:
TITLE: Periodic Performance Evaluation Review		NO: 5.4	PAGES:

(ii)   Preparation

Report preparation is important and ample time should be alloted to prepare the report.

a.   *Assignment Responsibilities and Circumstances*

The form is designed to obtain specific answers to questions, amplified as appropriate by description, comment or discussion.

Regarding the level at which the person was used on the assignment, indicate the level at which he or she functioned rather than the actual level. Criteria should include the nature of the work, degree of supervision and prior staffing of the assignments.

The nature of the work, for the auditor's major responsibilities, should be described in sufficient detail, for example: internal control (sales, cash receipts, payroll)—documentation, audit program, walk-through; inventory—observation, pricing finished stock; accrued liabilities—test for unrecorded liabilities. Unusually difficult or simple situations should be identified.

b.   *Manager/Director Approval*

This is required on all evaluations prepared by staff-level personnel, namely supervising senior, senior, et al. Approval should be indicative of Manager/Director concurrence with the evaluation (see Manager/Director comments section) and that it contains the appropriate information. When prepared by staff-level personnel, it is recommended that the report be read by the Manager prior to review with the individual. Manager/Director approval should occur after the report has been discussed with the individual and finalized. Any Manager/Director comments should be included in the evaluation at the time the individual signs off on the report.

c.   *Comments Section*

When completing this section, the auditor's experience level should be considered in evaluating his or her performance. For example, the criteria for measuring a staff auditor's technical skills would differ significantly from those used in evaluating a senior. It is expected that completion of all categories will generally be appropriate except for the Development of Assistants category for evaluations of staff auditors.

The boxes at the right margin are to be used to insert the abbreviation for the effectiveness level for each listed qualification. Effectiveness levels are defined on the last page. It is expected that everyone will become familiar with the definitions and use them as explained. Although OUTSTANDING and UNSATISFACTORY should be clearly explained, specific comments should also be given for other effectiveness levels for informative reporting to the auditor and the reader.

Areas noted for improvement should include any recommendations for the individual's development. In discussing weaknesses, the evaluation should assess the progress made in correcting those weaknesses during the course of the engagement. In situations when mitigating circumstances may have contributed to a weakness, appropriate details should be provided. However, it is not appropriate, for example, to discuss budget overruns when it clearly was not within the control of

204   5.4   Periodic Performance Evaluation Review

the individual. When one weakness impacts several qualification categories, the evaluation should clarify this so as not to mislead the reader into concluding that several weaknesses exist.

d. Appraisal Section

The last page of the report summarizes the results of the performance evaluations, both interim and end of assignment.

Where completing the sections dealing with Developmental Needs and Promotability, comments, reasons and recommendations should be expressed clearly and constructively to provide reliable source information to audit management for future assignments and indicated training and development needs.

Manager/Director Comments are required for all evaluations where that level of approval is necessary. The basis for approval may be discussions with the in-charge senior, review of workpapers or personal contact. The Manager or Director may also include here other significant comments.

The Summary Evaluation Section should be completed subsequent to the Comments Section and should be supported by the written comments. Since it represents a summary of the written comments, emphasis is again placed on the need to rate individuals on the basis of their experience level and standards normally expected at *that* level. In rating an individual's effectiveness level, the definitions provided on the form should be referred to. Ratings other than these should not be used. The most appropriate rating must be chosen. Written comments should explain borderline decisions.

(iii) Perfomance Appraisal Meetings

Performance appraisal meetings provide a very important opportunity to discuss and improve employee performance. This is a major element in a personnel development program. At every opportunity, the audit department culture should emphasize the importance placed on continuing personnel improvement and development. The audit department is only as good as the personnel performing the work. To the extent that employees performance can be improved, the overall quality of the audit products will be improved.

It is important that adequate time be allowed to plan for and conduct a performance appraisal meeting. The meeting should be scheduled with the employee to reduce the anxiety sometimes associated with performance appraisal meetings. All attempts should be made to create a comfortable atmosphere and reduce or eliminate interruptions. The performance meeting presents an opportunity to review progress and priorities, resolve any problems with performance and discuss future potential development needs and means to accomplish them. (Either through specific assignments or training addressing development needs.)

Conducting the performance review can be a challenging endeavor, and efforts should be made to train supervisory staffs to better conduct performance review meetings. During the meetings, it is important to create two-way communications. This involves getting the employee to open up. The evaluator will be prepared with his or her comments. The meeting atmosphere should be informal and unhurried. This can be accomplished by meeting in a conference room or away from a manager or supervisor's desk, if possible. It is also important to emphasize the good work that the employee has accomplished. There should be an emphasis on "praise" in the appraisal. It is important that the reviewer probe and ask questions, and most importantly, listen to the answers. This will provide ample time for the employee to discuss thoughts on his or her mind.

One of the objectives of the review process is to allow the employee to face up to the problem. In some cases, the best approach to mentioning the problem is to use the self-appraisal approach. Under the self-appraisal approach, the supervisor or manager will ask the employee to discuss his or her performance from their perspective. It is very important to always discuss performance and not the individual's personality. Any criticism should be made in a positive manner. For instance, talk about how they can improve.

There should be few surprises in the appraisal meeting. Problems should be discussed with the staff when they are recognized. This will allow the supervisor to correct the problem earlier and also demonstrate by example the existence of the problem. When this is not accomplished, specific examples should be raised during the appraisal review meeting. However, this is not as good an alternative as actually having mentioned the problems as they occurred.

Before the meeting is concluded, you should agree on a plan for action. Outline your thoughts on action points prior to the performance meeting. Focus on facts and avoid general judgments. Set objectives and goals and agree upon completion dates.

5.5 ANNUAL STAFF MEETING/CONFERENCE

As pointed out numerous times in this manual, personnel development is critical to the development and maintenance of a quality audit program. The Core and Advanced Personnel Development Programs are set out in Section 5.2, Personnel Development. One of the key programs in any audit department is the Annual Staff Meeting/Conference. The meeting has many objectives, including:

- Setting aside some time for department-wide administrative updates

- Discussions of company developments

- Audit training

- Reports on results of quality assurance reviews and related changes

- Provide a form for feedback communications from the staff and opportunities for suggestions for improvement of department operations.

The location of the meeting is very important to the overall meeting success. Meetings should be planned outside the office for a maximum impact. In addition, it may be combined with a social or sports activity to help build morale and camaraderie among the staff.

The program can include a State of the Department Address by the Chief Auditor. Presentations by department managers are also very important. Each functional leader should also provide an update on their administrative activities, including the Quality Assurance program and the Personnel Development program.

(a) Group Discussions

In order to provide a form for feedback from the staff, consideration should be given to holding group discussions. A sufficient amount of time should be allowed for group discussions considered a minimum of two hours. The staff should be broken down by groups, and these sub-groups should be provided with private meeting space to hold these discussions. The discussion should be open to any type of discussion initiated by the staff members. In order to organize the group discussions, a Group Discussions Instruction Sheet should be prepared. Figure 5.7 shows the Group Discussion Sheet for a potential meeting. The groups should have a Group Leader and a Scribe. The role of the Group Leader and the Scribe should be set out in the Group Discussions Instruction Sheet.

The Leader's role is to set the stage by informing the staff that this is their time and that they could talk about anything related to the department's organization or activities. The Leader should be provided with a list of some potential items of interest to generate conversation if necessary. However, there should be sufficient time allotted before this list is introduced to ensure that the staff

Figure 5.7   Group Discussions Instruction Sheet

Objective

- To provide a forum for the staff to discuss their concerns and hear other members' concerns.

- To provide feedback to Audit Management as to what are the main concerns of the staff and what possible solutions they project.

Group Leader's Role

- Set the stage by informing the staff that this is *their time* to talk about anything related to the Corporate Internal Audit Department's organization or activities. Tell them you have a list of some items of potential interest you will use to generate conversation when there is none or to improve the productivity of the conversation if its gets way off course.

  Explain that there is a scribe to take notes on what is said, not who said it, and that we will provide feedback later in the day.

  Ask the group to begin and wait a few minutes. Give the group a good chance to start on their own.

  Keep the meeting moving. If too much time is spent on a topic, ask to move onto another topic.

Scribe's Role

- Listen carefully and make notes of key concerns, suggestions, items of interest, etc. If you don't understand what someone is trying to say, ask questions to clarify the issue.

Observer's Role

- Listen in on a portion of each meeting.

Potential Topics

1. How important is audit planning? Is our approach adequate? How should we approach it?

2. Should we employ management by objectives and goal setting?

3. Should we require certification of some kind (CPA, CIA, CISA, CDP) within a given time frame?

Figure 5.7 Continued

4. How much of a factor should evaluations of performance be in determining raises and promotions?

5. Other:

   - Annual Staff Meetings

   - IS Audits/Training Participation in Audits

   - Job/Career Future

   - Audit Staff—Administrative Matters—Travel, Advances, Accommodations, etc.

has an opportunity to bring up their own thoughts and ideas. The role of the Scribe is to listen carefully and make notes of key concerns, suggestions and items of interest. This frees the Group Leader to concentrate on the Leader's role-keeping the meeting moving. The Scribe will produce a list which should be provided to audit management. The list should not indicate who made what recommendations.

In many group discussion meetings, an observer is also involved. The observer could be the Chief Auditor or Audit Management. Their role is to listen in on a portion of each meeting so as to gain an understanding of the temperament and direction of each meeting. The observer should not speak at any meeting. The purpose of the meeting is not to provide answers but to develop questions of interest and proposed solutions.

Group discussions require feedback from Audit Management. The Scribe's individual meeting summaries should be combined for review by Audit Management at a subsequent meeting or responded to at the conclusion of the Annual Staff Meeting/Conference. The sooner the feedback, the better. For instance, if simple issues or ideas are brought up that could be acted on immediately, these responses should be included in the closing remarks of the Chief Auditor. Those issues and suggestions which require more careful attention should be thought about and summarized in a memorandum of feedback to all participants in the Annual Meeting.

Annual Meetings can prove to be very productive if proper attention is paid to planning and arrangements.

5.6 NEW STAFF ORIENTATION

Welcome to Sam Pole Corporate Audit. We hope you find your position with us beneficial and rewarding. One of the first projects necessary to acquaint you with Sam Pole and Corporate Audit is orientation. Orientation is designed to formally introduce you to our company and significant department policies and procedures. A checklist has been provided to ensure your orientation is thorough and that you receive all materials. The checklist is to be signed off by you and the person making the orientation presentation. This form will be retained in your personnel file.

Many of these items may already have been discussed during your interview with Sam Pole. However, orientation will give you a more detailed explanation. We encourage you to ask questions; people on the staff will be happy to help you or many questions can be answered by reading the Procedures Manual. Please ask questions concerning matters about which you are not sure.

These welcoming remarks are often used when new personnel join the department. A sample orientation checklist can be found in Figure 5.8. A general description is provided here for each item on the orientation checklist.

Introduction to Staff

The person presenting the orientation will introduce you to members of the staff in the office. They will also identify those persons not present and provide you with a list of the staff in the audit division.

Facility

You will be given a guided tour of the Corporate Audit Department and other nearby facilities.

Parking

Parking will depend upon the division where you work. Additional parking facilities are available at a cost to you.

When you are in the field during your initial visit to the auditee's office, identify where you have parked and ask about their parking requirements.

Organizations

Organization charts of the Corporate Audit Department and the Corporation are in Chapter 1 of this manual.

SAM POLE COMPANY	LOGO	CORPORATE AUDIT DEPARTMENT	
		PROCEDURES MANUAL	DATE:
TITLE: New Staff Orientation		NO: 5.6	PAGES:

Figure 5.8   Orientation Checklist

	DATE	INITIALS
Introduction to Staff	_____	_____
Facility	_____	_____
Parking	_____	_____
Key Personnel	_____	_____
Organization Annual Report Issued	_____	_____
Employee Benefits	_____	_____
Job Description	_____	_____
Performance Evaluation Review	_____	_____
Three-Month Probation	_____	_____
Working Hours	_____	_____
Vacations	_____	_____
Sick Time	_____	_____
Personal Time	_____	_____
Time Reports	_____	_____
Travel	_____	_____
Cash Advances	_____	_____
Air/Rail Travel	_____	_____
Expenses	_____	_____
Keys (Sign Out)	_____	_____
Library	_____	_____
Data Processing Security/Badges	_____	_____
Professionalism	_____	_____
Procedures Manual (Read)	_____	_____
Safety Equipment Issues		
Hard Hat	_____	_____
Glasses	_____	_____

All items listed above have been explained to me, and I have no further questions at this time.

_____	_____	_____	_____
Orientation Supervisor	Date	Employee Signature	Date

Annual Report

You will receive the current annual report of Sam Pole Corporation. Key officials are identified in the annual report, along with major components of the Sam Pole organization. You should study this report thoroughly.

Employee Benefits

You will be issued employee benefit authorization cards which must be filled out and signed. You will be issued an Employee Benefits Manual. Read it carefully, and if you have any questions, discuss them with Audit Department management. If we do not know the answers, we will obtain them from the employee benefits office or refer you to the Human Resources Department.

Job Descriptions

Job descriptions are available in the Procedures Manual. Your job description will be carefully discussed with you during orientation. If you have any questions, please see the manager.

Performance Evaluation Reviews

The form that is used for performance evaluations will be discussed with you. It is contained in Chapter 5 of the Procedures Manual. Study the form; if you have any questions, please ask.

Three-Month Probation

All employees hired by the Corporate Audit Department are subject to a three-month probationary period. This is for the evaluation of initial performance.

Working Hours

Normally, the office hours are from 8 A.M. to 5 P.M. Monday through Friday. The exception to this is when auditing outside of your home location. If 40 hours can be accomplished Monday through Thursday by working 10-hour days, then at the discretion of audit management, you may return home Thursday night.

Auditing, however, is a concerted task-oriented profession. As professionals, when circumstances warrant, expect to spend the necessary additional hours to accomplish our objectives in a timely manner.

Salaries

Professionals employed by the Corporate Audit Department are salaried personnel. Overtime is not paid.

Vacations

The Corporate Audit Department follows vacation schedules as set forth in the Sam Pole Personnel Policy Manual.

Sick Time

The Corporate Audit Department will follow Corporate sick pay policy. If you are sick, you are to notify the office and the in-charge auditor as early as possible in the morning.

Personal Time

Personal time is provided for by the Corporate Policy providing three personal days per year. There are times when personal business, such as studying for certification exams, may be conducted during working hours if prior permission is obtained from the Manager, Corporate Audit.

Time Reports

Time reports are required on a semi-monthly basis. A form will be shown to you, and you will be instructed on how to complete it.

Travel

With audit locations situated away from home offices, there is a need for travel to these locations. For travel information, refer to the Corporate Audit Department Procedures Manual-Travel Policies.

Advances

Each division may make temporary cash advances for expenses. Advances must be shown on expense reports and accounted for monthly. Unused advances must be remitted to the company monthly.

Air/Rail Travel

Tickets for air/trail travel can be obtained from the travel department (and accounted for in the same manner as cash advances) or purchased directly by the auditor and reported on the expense report.

Expenses

Sam Pole has issued a pamphlet, "Reporting of Travel and Business Expenses," to be used with the exception of those items which are specifically provided for by the Corporate Audit Department.

Keys

The new employee will be given certain keys where appropriate. These must be signed out on the log maintained by the secretary at your location.

Library

The department office library contains various Sam Pole manuals. You should become acquainted with these manuals. Other publications available for education or research are also in the office library. They will be shown to you and also the checkout procedure applicable to the local offices (see Recommended Reading List).

Data Processing Security/Badges

Where badges are required, you will be evaluated on an as-needed basis before badges will be issued to you. This will be arranged through the Manager of Corporate Audit.

Professionalism

Corporate Audit is striving to make our department an outstanding department. A friendly, courteous relationship with auditees, outside auditors and other Sam Pole employees is paramount in having good public relations. We consider ourselves professionals and should act and dress accordingly. Dress should be in good taste. Try not to have extremes on either side.

Procedures Manual

The master manual is retained in the office; in-charge auditors have a copy to be used at the work sites. This manual was developed for the benefit of new employees and to document procedures to be followed. It is important to become familiar with the manual because we follow these procedures and are evaluated accordingly.

Safety Requirements

There are occasions when we must work in areas that require safety equipment. In most areas where equipment is required, the location will provide equipment. In the Division where visits to the factories are customary, the department issues a hard hat and safety glasses.

Chapter 6

QUALITY ASSURANCE AND MARKETING

6.1 QUALITY ASSURANCE
   (a) Objective
   (b) Responsibility
   (c) Method
       (i) Summarized Review of All Assignments by Unassigned Auditors
       (ii) Detailed Review of Selected Assignments
       (iii) Annual Self-Assessment of Department-Wide Standards, Policies, and Procedures
       (iv) Triannual External Review
   (d) Reports
       (i) Annual Report to the Audit Committee of the Board of Directors
       (ii) Annual Report to the Director of Auditing
       (iii) Selected Assignments Review
   (e) Summary of Review
   (f) Quality Assurance Checklist

6.2 MARKETING THE AUDIT FUNCTION
   (a) Introduction
   (b) What Is Marketing?
   (c) Understanding the Customers
   (d) Getting the Audit Message Out
   (e) Human Resources
   (f) Summary

6.1 QUALITY ASSURANCE

(a) Objective

The objective of the quality control program is to ensure that all assignments are completed in accordance with the department's and Institute of Internal Auditors' standards.

(b) Responsibility

It is the responsibility of the Director of Auditing to have quality audits completed on all assignments and to maintain a quality control program to evaluate the operations of the department.

The Director of Auditing will appoint a Quality Assurance Coordinator, who will be responsible for the quality control program and for keeping the Director of Auditing informed of all results.

(c) Method

The program is in four parts. They are:

1. Summarized review of all assignments by unassigned auditors

2. Detailed review of selected assignments

3. Annual self-assessment of department-wide standards, policies, and procedures

4. Tri-annual external review.

(i) Summarized Review of All Assignments by Unassigned Auditors

Objective

The objective is to ensure that all assignments meet minimum standards for planning, supervision, and documentation.

Responsibility

The manager on the engagement is responsible for ensuring:

- The workpapers are complete
- The work was properly planned
- The work was properly supervised
- The workpapers were properly reviewed.

It is the responsibility of the quality control coordinator to have all assignments reviewed for meeting of minimum department standards. He/she is also responsible for communicating the deficiencies noted to the audit manager and to follow up on correcting the deficiency.

Method

Unassigned auditors will be required to review assignments which they did not work on. The review will be completed by answering the questions in the quality control checklist. (See Figure 6.1 for checklist.) All "no" and "N/A" answers must be fully explained. The completed checklist, together with the workpapers are then forwarded to the quality control coordinator for follow-up.

The Quality Assurance Coordinator will review all deficiencies noted with the senior and the manager of the assignment. The manager is responsible to see that the deficiencies are corrected. Once all deficiencies are corrected, the Quality Assurance Coordinator will sign off on the engagement checklist.

(ii)   Detailed Review of Selected Assignments

Objective

The objective of this phase of the quality control program is to see that Corporate Audit work-papers:

- Support the conclusions reached
- Are efficient
- Are appropriate in the circumstances
- Comply with department and professional standards.

Responsibility

The selection of assignments to be reviewed will be made by the Quality Assurance Coordinator (see Figure 6.2 for criteria). He will assign the detail review of workpapers to two seniors, preferrably from different locations or groups.

Method

Workpapers will be reviewed in detail using a published checklist (if appropriate). All "no" answers will be reviewed with the manager and the senior in-charge. All noted items, or the fact that there are no items, will be reported to the Quality Assurance Coordinator in selected assignment review memoranda.

The Quality Assurance Coordinator will summarize all items noted in these reviews and prepare the selected assignments review memo to the Director of Auditing.

Figure 6.1   Quality Assurance Checklist

I. GENERAL

A. Is the General section complete? _____

B. Are the workpapers in a binder and ready for filing? _____

C. Are all review notes and pending matters complete and removed from the binder? _____

D. Are workpapers properly ordered? Do they contain indexes and lead sheets where appropriate? _____

E. Is the engagement checklist complete? _____

F. Have all employee evaluation forms been completed? _____

G. Was timely notice given to auditee? _____

H. Has the auditee response been:

   1. Received? _____

   2. Reviewed: By Manager?   By In-Charge? _____

II. REPORTING AND CONTROL SECTION

A. Audit Report

   1. Is a final copy included in the workpapers? _____

   2. Is the report in standard format? The following should be included:
     a. Introduction _____
     b. Profile and/or financial highlights _____
     c. Scope of audit _____
     d. Conclusion _____
     e. Summary _____
     f. Other comments _____
     g. Detailed recommendations _____

   3. Do the detailed recommendations contain the following five attributes?
     a. Statement of condition _____
     b. Criteria _____

Figure 6.1 Continued

    c. Cause   _____

    d. Effect   _____

    e. Statement of action   _____

4. Was the report issued timely? If not, is the reason explained on the report distribution worksheet?   _____

B. Is a copy of the year-end financials, or other meaningful reports, included?   _____

C. Summary Memorandum

    1. Is it completed?   _____

    2. Was it prepared by senior or other appropriate individual?   _____

    3. Does it contain the following:
        a. Audit objectives   _____
        b. Audit results   _____
        c. Auditee background information   _____
        d. Budgeted hours to actual hours analysis, and explanations of significant variations   _____
        e. Comments for subsequent audits, if applicable   _____

D. Manager Comments—Are all significant accounting and auditing problems fully documented?   _____

E. Working trial balance (for year-end financial audits)—is a working trial balance complete and cross-referenced to the supporting workpapers?   _____

F. Audit Planning Memorandum

    1. Was it completed prior to the audit field work?   _____

    2. Approved by manager and Director of Auditing?   _____

    3. Does it contain the following:
        a. Audit objectives   _____
        b. Background information   _____
        c. Financial highlights   _____
        d. Description of significant audit procedures   _____
        e. Budgeted audit hours   _____
        f. Timing of audit   _____
        g. Auditors assigned   _____

Figure 6.1 Continued

G. Audit Programs _____

    1. Are they complete? _____

    2. Are they approved by manager and senior? _____

    3. Are changes approved by manager and senior? _____

H. Fluctuation analysis—Has it been completed and are all significant fluctuations explained? _____

I. Time Budget _____

    1. Is it completed? _____

    2. Does it aggree to hours reported per semimonthly Corporate Audit progress reports? _____

J. Audit Recommendation Summary/Interim Recommendation Worksheet

    1. Is it complete? _____

    2. Are comments appropriately cross-referenced to detailed workpapers? _____

    3. Are all recommendations not included in detailed Report of Recommendations and Comments, explained? _____

K. Were prior audit reports included? Did the auditee implement the items noted? Have the comments been repeated in the current year's report? _____

L. Is the notice to auditee and other appropriate correspondence included in the binder? _____

M. Noted for Future Audits

    1. Has consideration been given to developing CAAPs? _____

    2. Are the significant comments included in the summary memorandum? _____

N. Is the closing conference documented? _____

Figure 6.1   Continued

III.   AUDIT WORKPAPERS

A.   Have they been properly reviewed, as evidenced by:

1.   All workpapers referenced?   _____

2.   All workpapers signed off?   _____

3.   Do all workpapers contain headings?   _____

4.   Do workpapers contain evidence of review?   _____

5.   Have internal controls been considered and, if appropriate, tested?   _____

6.   Are conclusions on major accounts or areas stated and
     properly supported?   _____

7.   Were all material adjustments approved by the senior and manager?   _____

8.   Do the workpapers include a final report copy?   _____

Figure 6.2   Selection of Assignments for Detailed Review

1. Audits and Special Projects would be selected to meet the following criteria:

   - Minimum 10 percent of all assignments

   - Minimum 10 percent of audit hours incurred during the year

   - At least one assignment for each senior or supervising senior

   - At least one of all types of audits:

     - Financial

     - Systems Review

     - Special Projects

     - Data Center audits.

2. Assignments will be selected at random, supplemented by the Quality Assurance Coordinator's judgment, to meet all of the above criteria.

(iii) Annual Self-Assessment of Department-Wide Standards, Policies, and Procedures

Objective

The objective of this review is to ensure that the department is in compliance with department, corporate, and professional (Institute of Internal Auditors) standards.

Responsibilities

The Quality Assurance Coordinator is responsible for completion of this review.

Method

The Quality Assurance Coordinator will compare the actual operating procedures of the department with the "Standards of Professional Practice of Internal Audit," and other corporate and department standards as appropriate. This will be accomplished through review of documentation, interviews, and actual experience. Upon completion, the Quality Assurance Coordinator will prepare the annual report to the Director of Auditing.

(iv) Tri-Annual External Review

Objective

The objectives of this review are to:

- Obtain an outside view of the department's performance versus professional and internal standards
- Obtain suggestions for improving operating efficiencies.

Responsibility

It will be the responsibility of the Director of Auditing, upon the recommendation of the Quality Assurance Coordinator, to have a triannual review performed.

Method

The method of review—public accounting, other internal auditors or an Institute of Internal Auditors team—will be decided upon a complete review of the alternatives. Items which must be considered, are:

- Cost
- Confidentiality of Sam Pole records

- Expertise in performing reviews
- Knowledge of business and operating environment.

(d) Reports

There are several key reports. They include:

- Annual Report to the Audit Committee of the Board of Directors
- Annual Report to the Director of Auditing
- Selected Assignments Review.

(i) Annual Report to the Audit Committee of the Board of Directors
This is a summarized report, prepared by the Director of Auditing, to the Audit Committee, on the quality control program and the results of the annual self-assessment.

(ii) Annual Report to the Director of Auditing
This is a summarized report of the quality control program for the year that includes results of the annual self-assessment, summary of deficiencies noted, and suggestions for improvement.

(iii) Selected Assignments Review
This is a summary memorandum and detailed checklist, enumerating the deficiencies and findings from the detailed review of selected audits, prepared for each assignment selected in the annual review process discussed below. This memo is first reviewed with the assignment manager and in-charge accountant before being given to the Quality Assurance Coordinator.

(e) Summary of Review

A summary is prepared by the Quality Assurance Coordinator, of the detailed deficiencies noted in the ongoing review of all workpapers. This memorandum is sent to the Director of Auditing and discussed with the entire staff during an annual meeting.

(f) Quality Assurance Checklist

Prepared by unassigned auditors, the checklist will be completed on all assignments after they have been approved for filing by the manager, and the report has been issued (see Figure 6.1 for a check-list). Upon completion, the checklist will be forwarded to the Quality Assurance Coordinator who is responsible for follow-up, to ensure the elimination of any deficiency noted.

6.2 MARKETING THE AUDIT FUNCTION

(a) Introduction

A series of books were published in the 1980s examining what made successful companies so successful. Strengths included an obsession with quality, building a family or families out of employee groups, sound long range planning, price value of products, and services and a closeness to the customer. The need to be close to the customer and driven to satisfying the customer were basic principles learned in business school, but maybe sometimes businesses or operations such as audit functions lose this focus.

Audit departments need to be addressing all of these areas of their operations. Should an audit department get close to customers? Who are your customers? Should they have marketing functions? Do auditors produce products? Within the limits of independence and objective review of operations and financial position the answers are yes. Who are your customers? There are many types and they may not all want the same products.

The objective of this section is to remind auditors to think about who their customers are, what products are produced and to attempt to improve the deliver of the products by using some basic marketing concepts.

(b) What Is Marketing?

A conventional definition of marketing includes all the steps to place a product in the hands of a consumer. Marketing should be involved when the product is being developed to consider who the different customers are and how the product should be delivered to each. For instance, the audit department produces audit reports. Who reads the audit reports? The answer may include divisional financial managers and controllers, divisional operations managers, the corporate financial managers and chief financial officer, the corporate managers and chief executive officers, the audit committee and the independent auditors. These are all customers and they may want different products.

The audit report is discussed in Section 4.1 and includes a two-level reporting process that allows for some product differentiation and divides the product logically to allow for different combinations for different customers. Marketing involves studying the customers wants and satisfaction with the product. Does the corporate CEO want the same level of detail as the divisional controller. There is a very good chance he or she does not.

The audit report product has been designed, as discussed in Section 4.1 to allow for a summary audit report and a detailed audit report. To respect the time commitments of the CEO type customer the summary report is limited to two pages. The reader of the summary report is always offered the full detailed report on request. To help differentiate this important report from others arriving on the customers desk, a color banner is suggested to highlight the product.

(c)   Understanding the Customers

Marketing requires understanding the needs of the customers and assessing their understanding of the product and their satisfaction with the product. Marketing and successful acceptance of the products can be enhanced by studying and understanding the customer's profiles including, age, background, time commitments, priorities, and need for information. For example, most financial managers have a financial background that enables them to understand more fully financial audit reports; however, corporate financial managers may not have the same time available for every division and may only want summary information on non-problem audit reports.

Operations managers may not understand as fully the implications of the audit findings. Consider adding a separate background report or glossary when applicable. To respect the time availability of customers and the need to commit the audit department to clear reporting of results, an opinion paragraph is included in the summary audit report. Some audit departments include a quantified score or grade for each audit. Therefore, by considering the customer, the audit departments adds value to their product by producing products they want and will be satisfied with.

(d)   Getting the Audit Message Out

In addition to audit reports, the audit department produces many products including all written reports such as: reports to the audit committee, reports to management and budget reports. The preparation of all reports should include the study and evaluation of the intended customer and how the product could be developed and delivered in a better, more comprehensive, and more highly productive way.

Audit department brochures are marketing tools that can help the department improve the understanding of the function and improve the image. This is a form of advertising, the objective of which is to show the product or service in a positive way while still respecting the professional image. The brochure becomes a recruitment tool as well as an orientation tool for new audit committee members and corporate and other senior management. The department brochure could include a message from the chief executive officer and the chief auditor and sections on audit department objectives and services, management's requests, who to contact, staff qualifications and organization, the role of the audit committee, what to do if a fraud is suspected and other important information.

Audit staff should be encouraged to be professionally active to develop professionally, gain solid knowledge of emerging developments and solutions, and to promote the audit department. High visibility in the audit profession will also enhance the audit department image. Reports on professional activities should be included in reports to management and reports to the audit committee. As discussed above these are different customers with different information needs which should be considered as the product (report) is developed.

Issuing control-related brochures to improve the organization's system of internal control can add value and reduce the negative reporting image of internal audit. For example a brochure on basic personal computer controls (Backups, password security, etc.) can improve individual employees' control awareness and improve the overall system of internal control. This approach markets the audit department in a positive way.

(e) Human Resources

As discussed in more detail in Chapter 5, audit departments are developers of people. The department can be used as a training ground for financial and operational managers. If this approach is taken, human resource development becomes a significant audit department product. To manage this program a summary should be kept of all audit personnel hired each year with information on promotions, transfers and separations. From this summary (see Figure 6.3) statistics can be developed on number of personnel transferred and promoted.

Using the audit department as a training ground also helps address the issues of career path opportunities for the audit department. It produces a tangible additional and positive audit product for the organization. Of course, it requires more work on the part of audit management. Planned turnover will result and staff scheduling becomes more complex. If the audit department is going to be used as a training ground a formal Management Development Training Program should be developed outlining the plan's objectives and guidelines.

(f) Summary

Marketing considerations are important elements in every business operation including the audit function. Constantly be on the lookout for opportunities to market the audit function and produce positive deliverables and new products and services.

Figure 6.3 Summary of Personal Activities

National Brand 45-604 Eve-Ease
45-304 2-Pack
Made in USA

Sam Pole Company
Corporate Audit Department
Summary of Personal Activities
January 1, XXXX to December 31, XXXX

	Prepared By	Date
Prepared By		
Approved By		

Date	Staff Name	Position	Personnel Code (1)	Activity New Position (If Applicable)
Jan. 2	Jon Jones	Staff Auditor		
Feb. 15	Betty Clark	Staff Auditor	P	Senior Auditor
Mar. 21	Peter Kardys		T	Controller
Apr. 15	Linda Dell	Staff Auditor	S	

Summary

				Cumulative Summary XXX - XXXX
Promotions		1		5
Transfers		1		3
New Hires		1		8
Separations		1		2

Personnel Activity Codes:

P = Promotion
S = Separation
T = Transfer

RECOMMENDED READING LIST

Internal auditing:

1. *Montgomery's Auditng*, 11th Edition, O'Reilly, Vincent, Murray B. Hirsch, Philip L. Defliese, and Henry R. Jaenicke, John Wiley & Sons, New York, NY, 1990.

2. *The Practice of Modern Internal Auditing*, by Sawyer, published by The Institute of Internal Auditors.

3. *Cashons Handbook for Auditors* by Cashon, Neuwirth, Levy, published by McGraw Hill.

4. *CADMUS' Operational Auditing* by Kowalczyk, published by John Wiley & Sons/The Institute of Internal Auditors professional book series.

5. *Internal Auditing Principles and Techniques* by Ratliff, Wallace, Loebbeccke and McFarland, published by The Institute of Internal Auditors.

Information systems auditing:

1. *The Handbook of IT Auditing* by Warren, Edelson & Parker, published by Warren, Gorham & Lamont.

2. *The Practitioner's Guide to EDP Auditing* by Mullen, published by The New York Institute of Finance.

3. *EDP Auditing Conceptual Foundations and Practice* by Weber, published by McGraw Hill.

4. *Computer Audit, Control and Security* by Moeller, published by John Wiley & Sons.

5. *Business Data Communications* by Fitzgerald, published by John Wiley & Sons.

6. *Systems Audibility and Control*, published by The Institute of Internal Auditors.

7. *Designing Controls Into Computer Systems* by Fitzgerald & Fitzgerald, published by Jerry Fitzgerald & Associates, Redwood City, CA.

8. *Computerized Information Systems (CIS) Audit Manual* by Lainhart & Donahue, published by The Information Systems Control Foundation.

9. *Auditing Computer Security* by Vallabhaneni, published by John Wiley & Sons.

DISK INSTALLATION INSTRUCTIONS

COMPUTER REQUIREMENTS

This product requires an IBM-PC or compatible computer with DOS version 3.0 or later. To read the forms you can use Microsoft Word 2.0 or WordPerfect Version 5.1. All of the forms and charts on the diskette are formatted in Microsoft Word 2.0.

If you have a different word processing package, consult your user manual for information on using Microsoft Word formatted files with your package. Most popular word processing programs are capable of reading files formatted in other word processing packages. Use the index in your software manual and refer to the section entitled *Loading Files from Other Programs.*

INSTALLING THE DISKETTE

The enclosed diskette contains 36 individual files in a compressed format. To use the files, you must run the installation program for the diskette. The default installation settings will create a directory on your hard drive called CANGEMI. It is under this directory that the forms and charts can be located.

To install the files, please do the following.

1. Assuming you will be using drive A as the floppy drive for your diskette, place the disk into your floppy drive and at the **A:\>** prompt type **INSTALL**.

2. The default drive and directory settings are **C:\CANGEMI**. If you wish to change the drive and directory names, you have the option to do so. The forms and charts will be installed under the main directory.

The files are now successfully installed onto your hard drive.

USING THE FORMS

The forms and charts on the enclosed diskettes are in Microsoft Word 2.0 format. Using this format, a number of different users with different word processing programs can read the disk. The files will also have the extension .DOC, signifying that they have been formatted in Microsoft Word 2.0.

READING THE FORMS INTO MICROSOFT WORD FOR WINDOWS

To read a file into Microsoft Word for Windows, follow these steps:

Load the Word for Windows program as normal.

1. When the Untitled document is displayed, select **OPEN** from the **FILE** menu.

2. The **OPEN FILE** dialog box will appear. At this box, make the appropriate selections for the drive and directory of the document you want to review. For instance, to open file **1-1.DOC** in the CANGEMI directory, you must select drive C:\ and the directory CANGEMI and then type **1-1.DOC** under the file name. Click OK to proceed. The file will immediately load into Microsoft Word for Windows.

3. Make your changes and revisions to the document.

4. To print the file, select **PRINT** from the **FILE** menu.

5. When you are through editing it, you should save it under a new name (to avoid overwriting the original file) before you quit.

READING THE FORMS INTO WORDPERFECT FOR WINDOWS

To read the files into WordPerfect for Windows, follow these steps:

Load the WordPerfect for Windows program as normal.

1. Select **OPEN** from the **FILE** menu.

2. The **OPEN** dialog will appear. At this box, make the appropriate selections for the drive and subdirectory of the document you want to review. For instance, to open the file **1-1.DOC** located in the CANGEMI directory, you must select the CANGEMI directory.

3. Under the **FILES** option on the left side of the dialog box, enter **1-1.DOC** as the file name.

4. The **CONVERT FILE FORMAT** dialog box will appear on screen with the option for MS WORD for WINDOWS 2.0, 2.0a, 2.0b highlighted. Click OK to proceed. The file will immediately load into WordPerfect for Windows.

5. Make your changes and revisions to the document.

6. To print the file, select **PRINT** from the **FILE** menu.

7. When you are through editing it, you should save it under a new name (to avoid overwriting the original file) before you quit.

Directory Name	File Name	Description
CANGEMI	1-1	Sample Corporate Audit Charter
	1-2	Interview Questionnaire for New Internal Auditors
	1-3	Sam Pole Company Organization Chart
	1-4	Sam Pole Corporate Audit Department Organization Chart
	1-5	The Institute of Internal Auditors
	1-6	Information Systems Audit and Control
	2-1	Corporate Audit Planning, Scheduling, and Staffing
	2-2	Sample Three-Year Audit Plan
	2-3	Time System Codes: Audit Type Codes and Task Code
	2-4	Sample Corporate Audit Time Summary Form
	3-1	Corporate Audit Performance Process Matrix
	3-2	Sam Pole Company Corporate Audit Department Assignment Checklist
	3-3	Sample Notice to Auditee
	3-4	Sample Planning Memo
	3-5	Recommendation Worksheet Example
	3-6	Permanent Files Index
	4-1	Corporate Audit Reporting Process Matrix
	4-2	Transmittal of Report Draft to Audit Entity
	4-3	Transmittal of Report Draft to Senior Financial Officials
	4-4	Overdue Response to Audit Report: 30-Day Letter
	4-5	Delinquent Response to Audit Report: 60-Day Letter
	4-6	Transmittal of Policy on Reports of Public Accounts
	4-7	Audit Response
	4-8	Lead Paragraph Example
	4-9	Corporate Audit Report
	4-10	Corporate Audit Detail Recommendations and Comments
	4-11	Report to Management Example
	4-12	Report to Audit Committee
	5-1	Overview of Corporate Audit Training Model
	5-2	Continuing Professional Education Record
	5-3	Corporate Background Information Form
	5-4	Corporate Interest Questionnaire
	5-5	Performance Evaluation Review Form
	5-6	Group Discussions Instruction Sheet
	5-7	Orientation Checklist
	6-1	Summary of Personal Activity

USER ASSISTANCE AND INFORMATION

John Wiley and Sons, Inc. is pleased to answer questions regarding the installation program or a damaged disk. If you have any problems with installation please call our technical support number at (212) 850-6194, weekdays between 9 A.M. and 4 P.M. Eastern Standard Time.

To place additional orders or to request general information about orders or other Wiley products, please call Wiley customer service at (800) 879-4539.

INDEX